D0912097

Learning Golf's Essential Elements

By

Jim Howe

authorHOUSE®

AuthorHouse™
1663 Liberty Drive, Suite 200
Bloomington, IN 47403
www.authorhouse.com
Phone: 1-800-839-8640

First published by AuthorHouse   1/10/2008

ISBN: 978-1-4343-5173-9 (sc)

Printed in the United States of America
Bloomington, Indiana

This book is printed on acid-free paper.

Dedicated to my mother and
the memory of my father, Donald Howe

Introduction

Hitting a great golf shot certainly is one of life's pleasures. The feeling of solid contact between club and ball, then the sound made by that solid contact, are rewarding in themselves. But the elation from the sight of the ball traveling toward the intended target is hard to describe to the non-golfer. This simple pleasure, although occasionally experienced by some, is usually reserved on a consistent basis for those who either grew up in the game or have dedicated the time necessary to develop an efficient golf swing. For beginning to intermediate golfers, or perhaps late bloomers who have just discovered the career benefit of playing the game, there are just enough pleasures during a round of golf or a trip to the driving range to counterbalance their own perception. Usually that perception is that the only reason they continue to play is that they are gluttons for punishment.

You may be that non-golfer, or you may be have occasionally had that great shot experience. You may be a businessman or businesswoman who needs to learn the game to benefit your career. Perhaps you are a student who has little time or money but has the desire to play, or you want to understand and have a blueprint to develop your ability. Whether you belong to one of the groups just described or to one of many other categories, I am sure the book you are holding can help. It can help you have that great shot pleasure on a more consistent basis, creating more enjoyment of the game.

Trying to hit a golf ball can be a frustrating experience. But why the struggle, why the frustration? The ball isn't even moving. It's not like you are on a polo pony traveling at breakneck speed and swinging the mallet under the neck of the horse trying to pass the ball to another person doing the same. Nor are you trying to hit a Nolan Ryan fastball, a pitch that could possibly take your head off if it happened to be errant. Now, those are hard! Hitting a golf ball should be easy compared with those two experiences.

Through my education and work as a golf instructor at Cal State University–Fullerton, and as a teaching professional, I have experience in teaching thousands of students, in every situation from the classroom to the private lesson. The material in this book emanates from these experiences, as well as from my own time spent learning to play the game. Because I am continually around people who are struggling with their games, I am constantly reminded of my own early efforts. I recall much of the well-intended advice that I received, and I can't forget the frustration of hitting a great shot one minute and a horrible shot the next.

There are thousands of tips and tidbits of advice to help the underachiever hit more decent shots while challenging the golf course. These tips are in books, magazines, and even late-night infomercials; there is spousal advice, friendly advice, and perhaps some not-so-friendly advice from playing partners. "Change your grip; master the short game; putt with soft hands; shorten the backswing" are all common critiques. Advice, even when well intended, is often damaging for the beginning golfer, because it is either wrong or delivered at the wrong time in the golfer's stage of development. If improving the golf game were as simple as assimilating and incorporating tidbits of "friendly advice," there would be far more golfers playing the game for a living. I have come to the conclusion that trying to incorporate random advice into your swing won't help you eliminate inconsistency or improve your game.

What about trying scientific theory? Very few people I know have that kind of time. Classic scientific theory requires holding the number of variables steady, changing only one at a time to isolate the "problem." Golf is more like a Rubik's Cube than a scientific experiment. Just today on the Internet I read about a six-year-old child who solved a jumbled cube in just 37.89 seconds. Maybe that kid should take up golf. My friend Cory, who was most helpful to me in finishing this book, told about his favorite movie, *Jurassic Park*. His hero is Jeff Goldblum, who plays the part of a chaos theorist. He's the nerd explaining chaos theory to the gorgeous female lead, and the entire time Cory is thinking the guy should become a golf teacher. Goldblum turns his hand over, drops a bead of water on his knuckle, and tells the woman to watch how the water runs off his hand. It runs left. He repeats the experiment with another drop of water placed in exactly the same spot on his hand. This time it runs off the right side. He explains that "any little hair, wrinkle, or muscle will change ever so slightly to alter the path of the water," and thus explains chaos theory. Now, THAT'S golf. The wind, the soil, your hands, the moisture, your concentration, and your muscle contractions can all alter the club path and throw your swing into complete chaos.

There is no scientific trial and error for the average golfer. There's just not enough time or ability to isolate the variables when you play twice a month. Chaos theory can and will take over for the beginner or intermediate player. Only the pros or those with equal time and talent have a fighting chance of using scientific theory to rule out bad habits and a thousand buckets of balls, in as many practice sessions, to groove good ones. Therein lies the purpose of this book.

First, this book should help you have realistic expectations for changing your results rather than create unrealistic expectations that your results will change. In a word, this book should help you do the best you can with the science of the game given your time "in the lab" to carry out the experimentation. That's this book's primary golf advice. If you expect to become a professional by reading this (or any) book, changing all kinds of variables and practicing infrequently enough to torture yourself, you'll only end up frustrating yourself out of the game. If you want to stick around, you'll need to learn more than a good golf swing. You'll need to enjoy hitting more good shots than bad, and enjoy holding your own with customers (and/or total strangers) as a knowledgeable connoisseur of the game. If you're a minimalist looking to quickly identify only what you need to learn and how much is necessary to become a competent and credible player, and you are forced to learn and practice it just about anywhere but the golf course, then this book will help you succeed. You'll need help not only with the swing, but also with etiquette, rules, and the vocabulary of the game.

Vocabulary is essential to the game. It drives me crazy when someone uses the word *golf* incorrectly. "I golfed yesterday" or "I golfed with him once." The word *golf* is a noun, not a verb. When someone offers to "pull the stick out of the hole before I shoot my ball," I cringe. Avoiding embarrassment might begin with learning how to "talk the game." You will find necessary words and phrases throughout the book as well as a glossary at the end.

A working knowledge of the rules is paramount. You don't need to know every rule, just the common ones. I find it curious when people study the rule book for that one obsequious and rare rule for a ball that has lodged in the gullet of a pelican. Knowledge of outrageous rules should be left to the PGA official, whom the player can call on in a tough situation. Like a lawyer, a golfer need not memorize every law if there is a library full of legal precedents just down the hall.

And finally, etiquette is the key to avoiding embarrassment, and is our playing partner's yardstick for measuring our golf prowess and inner soul. Dan was in the oil business and was a hardnosed, nononsense businessman. I gave him golf lessons for several years and learned that he wanted me to be tough on him during our sessions and to be honest with him about his progress as a golfer. During this time we became friends, and I value his advice even today. He told me a story one day about a young man who tried to solicit business from him on the golf course. Dan said he was taken to a very expensive golf course overlooking the ocean. The young man had the best equipment and dressed the part of a golfer. It was obvious to Dan that he had practiced hard on his golf swing, both because he hit the ball quite well and because he told Dan he had practiced hard on his golf swing. Dan would have been very impressed except for the fact that this young man had little sense of the proper etiquette of the game. In fact, his etiquette was so bad that Dan found it downright distracting. He stood in the wrong places, spoke at the wrong times, and even improved his lie and fudged his score. From where Dan sat, this lack of etiquette revealed the young man's true moral fiber. Given a choice, Dan would do business with someone whose company he enjoyed and whom he could trust. The young fellow's intent on learning the golf swing, without concern for the rules and etiquette of the game, actually cost him Dan's business.

It is my experience that golfers who understand the golf swing and the game of golf will have the opportunity for faster and longer-lasting improvement, embarrass themselves less, improve their confidence, and enjoy the game. This book not only is about learning the golf swing, but also includes the other essential elements that are necessary to be considered a golfer by your peers, your customers, and total strangers. Knowing the proper amount of etiquette and the more common and basic rules and having a few key aspects of the swing to master just about anywhere will allow you to play and enjoy the game with anyone at almost any level.

I have stopped and started, written and rewritten this book many times over the years. Finally I feel confident that it is in a format that will benefit you as you strive to become a golfer. Included are many stories about my experiences of learning to play and teaching the game. Many of these stories are humorous, but all are of struggles and successes that people have had in learning to play.

I have been playing this game for more than forty-five years and still continue to learn. It seems like it is a never-ending process, and I am sure it always will be that way. It is the same with this book. It is not the final and complete answer. No matter how much information is included, there could have been more. This book, however, will give you a foundation to help you develop your game and a reference as you progress.

Table of Contents

Chapter

Learning

Golfers often have trouble relating learning the golf swing with learning other skill movements. I certainly have fallen into that category on occasion. My gymnastics experience is a great example of that, because it was certainly not my favorite sport when I was younger. But now that my daughter is becoming a more and more proficient gymnast, it is becoming one of my favorite sports to watch. This may seem like an odd beginning to a golf book, but I believe you will see my point.

I disliked the gymnastics class I took in college primarily because it was very difficult for me. The reason I found it so difficult was that I could never seem to keep my balance, which is not only a key component in gymnastics but critical. One of the reasons I couldn't keep my balance was that I never let myself get off balance. I was too rigid, too intent on doing exactly the right thing, and wouldn't let myself fall down. In other words I wouldn't do what it took to learn balance.

I have watched my daughter since she was a little girl doing cartwheels and handsprings. If she fell down, which happened frequently, she simply got back up and tried it again. She actually learned balance by falling down. I have watched her and her teammates move up the ranks as competitive gymnasts and observed how they learn one skill, which leads to the next, more complicated skill. No Level Four gymnast (beginning competitor) would attempt the routine of a Level Ten (advanced) gymnast without learning the appropriate skills at each stage along the way. Not only could they not perform the more difficult routine, but it would be dangerous.

Learning the golf swing is not the same as learning gymnastics. Few people fall down during a swing at a golf ball, so the physical penalties for mistakes are not the same. Both, however, are motor skills. With any motor skill people acquire the ability to perform in much the same manner. There is a progression through a series of steps. These steps contain errors. The errors should be expected, accepted, and corrected before moving to the next level.

After observing thousands of students over the years I see this as an area in which many golfers fail. It appears to me that golfers do not feel as though they should go through the procedures of learning. Instead they simply should be able to perform, thus creating expectations that more often than not far exceed their ability. These expectations slow down the development of the golf swing if not stifle it altogether.

Years later it has become clear to me why I had so much trouble in my attempts at gymnastics, thus creating my dislike for the sport. It is too bad that no one made me aware of the process of learning balance, because even a small background in the sport would have been helpful to me as an aspiring golf professional. The flexibility, strength, and discipline that it takes to become a gymnast would have proven to be a great benefit to my golf game.

I saw learning balance in a real-life situation during a private lesson series. This was a series in which I was giving instruction to a very brave lady who told me that when she started to fall down, I should just let her fall. She had recently had surgery on her eardrum, creating a loss of equilibrium. The only way for her to relearn balance was to fall down. I witnessed this when she bent over to put the ball on a tee. It was very difficult to watch her, but it was a great example of why falling or failing to stand was critical in her relearning process.

In this chapter we will take a look at how people learn motor skills and specifically golf skills. Words that describe the golf swing and some of the myths of the golf swing are included as well.

Learning Skills

There are thousands of motor skills. Eating is a motor skill, as is playing golf. For many of us the golf swing is slightly more important that eating but obviously not as crucial to our health.

I became friends with a gentleman who had a vast knowledge and appreciation of the game of golf. He had taken lessons from some of the great golf instructors of all time, such as Percy Boomer and Earnest Jones. Alex and I had wonderful conversations. Even after he became sick and had to undergo surgery, he continued to practice and play. One day he complained to the doctor that the medication he was taking was affecting his motor skills. The doctor told him that the medication was helping to keep him alive. He replied, "But you don't understand: the medicine is ruining my putting stoke. Get me off of it!" Not many people take the game that seriously, but it does require motor skills, and many things affect our motor-skill abilities.

What is a motor skill? By definition a motor skill is any muscular activity that is directed toward a specific objective.

How do people learn motor skills? People learn motor skills by interpreting feedback. Feedback is the information that they receive while performing some type of movement.

Two very important variables in interpreting feedback are Knowledge of Results (KR) and Knowledge of Performance (KP).

Knowledge of Results is some representation of the actual outcome obtained. Examples would be the sight, sound, and feeling of a golf shot. A golfer tops the ball and interprets that shot as bad, most often making corrections for the next shot. A basketball player shoots a free throw that is short, so he puts more force into his next attempt.

Knowledge of Performance is analyzed by someone other than the performer. An example would be a golf instructor analyzing the golf swing for the golfer and verbalizing this observation. The instructor watches a student top a ball and tells the student the reason(s) he or she hit that type of shot. Instruction is then given about how to improve the next shot. The coach tells the basketball player who shoots the free throw short to bend his knees more.

Knowledge of Results and Knowledge of Performance are critical in learning the golf swing. Lack of understanding may delay, hinder, or even make developing the golf swing difficult. Why is that? Because in golfers' attempts to hit good shots they will make any swing adjustment that will work. By *work* I mean a better golf shot, not necessarily a better golf swing. Often the swing adjustments are just corrections upon corrections. Someone can certainly hit a good shot with a bad swing as well as a bad shot with a good swing.

That is one reason it is important for the student to understand the mechanics of the golf swing and even more important to have a teacher who understands and can explain the feedback from golf shots. Listening to well-intended advice on the driving range more than likely will prove to be a setback. The main reason is that unless the advisee is knowledgeable and has an understanding of the proper feedback, it is difficult to make the proper change.

One of my students was a very nice lady who was learning the game at a later stage in life, so her expectations were quite modest. Arriving for a particular lesson she was almost in tears. She had been practicing at a local driving range and was badgered by a fellow who had offered his unsolicited advice. Most of the advice contradicted our previous lesson. That lesson was based on a drill that was not intended to produce a good golf shot but was one in which we used Knowledge of Results to help develop a certain motion. This was a motion that at her age and physical stature was important. He was very insistent and would not leave her alone, and because she was such a nice person, she suffered through the session.

Our solution to the problem was to write a card asking questions of the gentleman's background as a teacher, what his intentions were for her game, and several more that only a true teacher would be able to answer. She laminated this card and the next time handed it to her so-called instructor. After reading it he handed it back and left. She kept it in her bag for future well-intended instructors.

Learning Golf Skills

Do you ever wonder how the golfers you watch on TV became so skilled? They are all individuals who developed a high skill level not only from different backgrounds, but from different parts of the world. With only a few exceptions these golfers have many common traits in the developmental stages of their golf swing.

Almost all golf professionals begin playing the game as youngsters. They began playing at a time in their lives when their bodies were physically developing, when they had little in the way of physical inhibitions, and most important, when time to practice was plentiful.

Most become very adept at the short game first. They become good golfers through their ability to score. Practice on the short game also helped them develop the proper touch and feeling needed in the full swing. There are many examples of this, but one that immediately comes to mind is Tom Kite. He happens to be from my era, and I have followed him for many years because I have admired his hard work. As an amateur and in the early stages of his professional career his short game was ahead of his golf swing—enough so that it carried him until all of his dedication and work on his golf swing began to pay off. As we know, he developed a tremendous golf swing and is one of the great players of all time.

Consistent in the development of these highly skilled golfers is the fact that they progressed through stages. It would be very hard to imagine that any golf professional went from beginner to advanced without many, many hours of practice and hundreds of rounds of golf. They may have progressed in a shorter time frame than most people, but still, there had to be a progression of skill. Their skill is the combination of physical ability, practice, and experience.

As I said, this skill may have taken them less time to develop, but it still required an abundance of time. Of all the factors required to develop a high skill level, this generally is the one adult golfers do not have. I can't emphasize this enough; in fact, understanding this may be the most important thing you can do to help yourself improve. Unless you have the same amount of time that it takes a highly skilled golfer to learn the game, you will not reach their skill level. Accept that and you will be better off than most people who challenge the game.

How does the average person learn a motor skill that takes even highly talented individuals years to develop? As I said earlier, learning to play golf takes more time than most people have. So the answer may be that the average person needs a method for learning that is different from that used by the highly talented players who perform on TV. Simple trial and error takes too much time. A person must learn how to interpret feedback and adjust their swings accordingly. Learning to interpret feedback is a skill in itself and also requires time to learn.

A method must be developed that is very specific and takes into consideration the amount of time that is available for practice. The average golfer must learn to analyze and use feedback properly. Earlier I wrote that Knowledge of Results and Knowledge of Performance are both critical to learning a motor skill. The person who does not have a great amount of time can learn the golf swing if that time is used wisely. Understanding and learning the underlying fundamentals of the golf swing along with understanding KR and KP is the best use of your time. Later in this book we will develop routines for you to do exactly that.

One of the more successful students with whom I have worked was very disciplined in his practice. Dave was just a beginner and not a very good one when he first began taking lessons. He acknowledged the fact that he did not have a lot of time to devote to wasted practice. In our lessons together we developed drills and routines that took his time into consideration. As he developed a consistent swing, he began working on his game on the golf course and eventually into tournament play through a club of which he was a member. In a few years his handicap had dropped to as low as 9. Dave now plays a very enjoyable and respectable game of golf.

There are only a few reasons that a person cannot learn to play a good game of golf. The key is the proper attitude toward your ability, toward your goal in relation to your time, and toward a specific practice.

Golf Words of Description

It is very difficult to describe something without using words. The golf swing is certainly no exception. But whose words do you use? I can say the same words to three different students and have them interpret them in three entirely different ways.

Often I hear people say how confusing magazines and books can be and that they have quit reading them because they tend to harm their golf swing. The problem is rarely in the content of the article or book. The author almost always is very knowledgeable on his or her subject. The problem is that the writer cannot possible know how a person will interpret the words. He or she may be most accurate in describing the motions of the golf swing, but will the reader be on the same level as the words were intended?

I was giving a lesson to a person who was involved with education. His job was to teach teachers how to be more effective. One subject that we discussed was the fact that good teachers take on the vocabulary of their students instead of the opposite. He made me aware that this was a powerful tool to use in golf instruction.

Since that time I have tried to understand the swing in the manner that students understand. I then try to describe the motions the way

I think the students would describe them. I believe this has improved my effectiveness as a golf instructor.

In writing it is a little more difficult. I certainly am not able to hear the reader talk, so changing my words for each individual reader is impossible. I have tried, however, to think as a student and to use words and phrases as I think most students would use the words and phrases.

An example of a word that I try to avoid is *turn*. This word is commonly used in describing the backswing, but it is one that I find particularly confusing. Few people who use it in this manner seem to move the way that it was intended. The key in the proper use of the word *turn* is the amount and the angle at which the body is in relation to the ground. It is a very difficult thing to verbalize, so unless I am working with a student who understands the concept, I do not use the word.

Quite a few years ago a very popular book was on the market, and it was easy to see which of my first-time students had read it. The contortions that they made on the backswing were a direct result of how the word *turn* was used frequently in the book. I thought this was my imagination, but other instructors with whom I worked were having the same experience with their students.

After reading the book I could understand what the author was trying to say because teaching the golf swing was my business and I had studied it most of my life. I could also understand why my students were so confused. The backswing turn that was described in the book was one that a skilled golfer should use, yet the book inferred that everyone should swing in the same manner. The author had assumed that the golfers reading the book had a reasonable if not high level of skill, and his words were intended for that golfer.

In defense of the author, as I suggested earlier, it is most difficult to write and know the correct words to use. I would guess that if each one of the people who read the book had taken the same instruction from the author in person, he would have been able to explain his point in a manner that would have been clear. I can't tell you how many times I have had to use words to describe the golf swing that were almost the opposite of those I would normally use. The reason is that I had to match the description of the swing to fit the student's ability and level of understanding.

Pictures, especially action pictures, can also be misleading. "A picture can be worth a thousand words" is an expression that I use often. However, like words spoken at the wrong time, they may prove to be a detriment to learning. In this book you will find no pictures because my word descriptions must be clear, precise, and accurate, thus giving you the proper mental picture, which I believe will be more beneficial.

I have used video in my lessons since 1979. At that time video recorders were very large, and it would take me a long time to set up for a lesson. Video is very valuable not so much for seeing what is wrong but for letting students describe in their own words what is correct. Oftentimes when making a swing golfers are not producing the motion they believe they are attempting. When they are shown the video, they are able to verbalize much better than I can what the swing actually felt like.

The Words of Grace. How important are the correct words? When I first moved to California, I met a lady named Grace. She was a very prim and proper person. Nothing was out of place in any part of her life except playing golf, which was beyond her control. She was taking lessons against her will (she had an insistent husband) and was very nervous. As we got to know each other, she relaxed a little, and one day out of nowhere came a series of nice golf shots.

Thinking it was a result of something profound I had said, I asked what key word, phrase, or thought from my incomparable instruction had made the difference. Her answer put me in my place. She said she had been thinking about a deli across the street where I could purchase a healthful sandwich. Well, it worked for her and it worked for me also, because it was a good deli! What did it have to do with the mechanics of the golf swing? Nothing at all! But thoughts and words like that made her relax, which was much more important than any word or even accurate description of the mechanics of the golf swing.

Dispelling Myths

While we are on the subject of words, let's dispel a few of the myths in the golf swing that might hinder your development. Bob Toski and Jim Flick in their book *How to Become a Complete Golfer* wrote about three long-standing myths. This book was written years ago, but these myths are still around and more often than not hinder the development of the golf swing.

Keep Your Head Down. This advice has been around forever. Probably it came about because of the fact that if you watch a good golfer, the head is indeed down and he or she appears to be looking at the golf ball at impact.

But watch a golfer's head immediately after the person hits the ball and you will see that it moves as the body rotates. It is human nature to watch the object that we are about to strike; it would be extremely unusual not to do so. In fact the golf swing happens so swiftly that I doubt many of us are capable of looking up.

The problem lies not in keeping your head down, but in new golfers' effort to do so. They limit the freedom of the flowing movement required to develop the golf swing. Keeping the head down is actually a very advanced technique!

Left Arm Straight. What is *straight*? To the beginning golfer *straight* means stiff. Tension in the golf swing is a killer. A person is far better off in the early stages developing a free-flowing swing and bending the left arm slightly. Arm extension will come with experience.

Straight Shots. Inexperienced golfers seem to be obsessed with straight golf shots. In fact, a common expression is that first they would like to hit the ball straight, then learn to hook and slice. If you sit back and think about it realistically, a straight shot is extremely difficult. Tournament players do not play the ball straight. It is far easier to play a ball that curves slightly, and in fact the fastest improvement will come when the golfer learns to hook the ball.

How Much Can Be Learned?

How much can one learn or be taught about the golf swing at any one time? How many different things can a person think about and still hit the golf ball? There is probably no answer to either question, because everyone learns differently.

Far too often golfers try to do too much and do it too quickly. They try to think of all the tidbits of advice and try to improve ball striking immediately. They also expect those teaching golf to give the answers to all problems and correct their swing instantly.

Physical swing changes will not automatically give immediate successful results. For example, if a golfer is accustomed to making too short of a backswing and the correction is to lengthen the stroke, surely that is going to give a different feeling and will affect the swing position before contact with the ball.

The golf shot itself will be affected until the change has been given time to evolve into the swing. Initially the shot may travel to the right. That is why the feedback needs to be interpreted correctly. If a person did not understand that the result of a particular swing correction may cause the ball to travel to the right, they may change back or away from the proper swing.

Craig was a very good player, and I have been paired with him a number of times in tournament play. One day he arrived at the first tee looking bewildered. He had gone to practice at a nearby range when an instructor walked up and began giving him unsolicited advice—so much advice that Craig had too many swing thoughts and absolutely no confidence.

So how much can a person learn at one time? A calculated guess on my part is that during practice a person can focus on only one change or new movement at a time. Practice should be centered on a specific routine that has a purpose, and that purpose is to make a positive swing change. Sometimes that swing change produces results that show good shots immediately. Sometimes the change produces poor shots.

I learned a format years ago while taking a class at Cal State–Fullerton. My movement anatomy professor was one of my favorites for several reasons but mainly because he explained complicated motions in practical terms. One of our assignments was to take a skill movement such as the golf swing and do a cinemagraphic segmental analysis. In other words you filmed a beginning golfer and compared the swing at different positions with that of an advanced golfer. It would have been an easy assignment if I had been allowed to use golf words, but unfortunately anatomical descriptions and phrases were required—terms such as *plantar flexion, extension,* and *inward rotation.* I had to compare motions of the knees, shoulders, hips, and even feet and in all three phases of the swing. It was an eye-opening experience and one that gave me a very different way to view the golf swing. I was able to adopt this paper into my own lesson plans and for years have done very much the same thing. I videotape individual students, explain the error or errors, let them see the difference in a model swing, then develop a practice plan to correct the errors.

How many errors do I point out and try to correct? It depends on the student but generally only the biggest error. Then we work on one change at a time and learn the effects that the change will have on his or her shot production.

The leaky dam theory. Golfers are like people trying to plug a leak in a dam only to discover that another leak has appeared. The golfer sometimes makes a correct swing change only to observe that the change has caused another error. What can be done? Become adept at the change regardless of the outcome, and once it has been mastered, move to the next change. The great teacher Percy Boomer in his book *On Learning Golf* put it best: **"Let the change in your swing take place irrespective of immediate results."**

Chapter

The Student

The definition of *student* is one who studies or investigates. A golf student, then, is practically everyone who takes up the game, because we all have to study it in some form or another. For many the study of the golf swing becomes a hobby and even a passion unto itself.

As with any other endeavor there are different types of students. There are good and bad, serious and less serious, fast and slow students. Some are visual, some are auditory, some are able to imitate, and others cannot.

I am often asked if I've ever had a student who could not learn or whom I told to quit. In thirty-five years of teaching I have only had one golfer to whom I suggested quitting the game.

Wild Walt. Many years ago Walt came to me for lessons. Walt was definitely not a student in any sense of the word. He had very little experience; thus his skill level was not high. That would have been okay, but he refused to accept that fact. His goals were to hit every shot straight and far, and to avoid going through any of the steps of learning the golf swing. He had physical problems that dictated he should swing the club in a certain manner, which he refused to do. He also had a job that restricted his practice time to a few hours each week. Taking all this into consideration Walt still could have learned to play. It just would have taken a very disciplined and organized practice method.

One day Walt was included in a group that was taking a playing lesson. The final straw between Walt and I came on the thirteenth hole, a par 3 over water. The pin was placed on the right side of the green, which meant that it would require a carry over the water. I suggested to the group that they play to the safe part of the green and not take the chance of bringing the hazard into play.

The whole group, including me, took the advice—everyone that is, except Walt. As usual he would not pay any attention and insisted on hitting the shot toward the flag. After he hit four shots into the drink, I had had enough. I suggested that he take his clubs and golf cart, follow the cart path to the clubhouse, and wait for us in the lounge. I would be happy to pay for his lunch and drinks, but I thought that maybe golf was not the game for him. Walt for the first time in weeks agreed with me and took off.

The rest of the group continued to play. We were standing on the fourteenth green when all of a sudden Walt showed up. He had taken the wrong turn, become lost, and circled the golf course. Walt asked if he could rejoin the group. We let him, and he played the rest of the way in with us without any difficulties. Walt gave himself a par on the thirteenth and fourteenth holes and was ecstatic when his score totaled up to one of his best ever. I never saw Walt again. I am sure he took up another sport, but I just hope it wasn't hunting.

You do not have to be a great student to learn the game of golf. But what you need to do is understand that you are a student and that learning takes place in an order. That order is not excellent to poor but actually the opposite. Again, if you are like most people, you probably don't have the time for trial and error, so be open minded and patient.

Like other parts of the book this chapter is subjective, and you have the right to change any word or phrase. These are my attempts at describing different skill levels, goals for the game, and limitations that may restrict learning. It is up to you to identify which are appropriate for you.

Description of Skill Levels

I believe it is important for you as the student golfer to identify your skill level. I will suggest four categories: beginning, beginning intermediate, intermediate, and advanced.

The skill level of a golfer depends on several things: feel for the club as it moves through the swing, control of the club, and the resulting golf shot. To a degree score is also an indication of a golfer's ability. The attainment of skill level as mentioned previously is a combination of natural ability, practice, and experience.

The following are sample descriptions of the four categories:

Beginner. This is a golfer with no experience or only slight experience. He or she may have played once or twice but has no well-defined swing.

Beginning Intermediate. The golfer who has played has some understanding of etiquette, hits erratic golf shots, doesn't have a very well-defined swing, and scores more than 100 on a regulation course.

Intermediate. Golfer who has moderate to extensive experience, golf swing is well defined, scores range from above 100 to low 80s, finds improvement quite slow. Most golfers generally stall out in the intermediate phase.

Advanced. A golfer with extensive experience and a single-digit handicap. This golfer has a well-developed swing that may even have errors, but through practice the player has learned to compensate.

As a golfer improves, he or she should progress from one stage to the next. It would be very difficult to imagine a person going from beginner to advanced golfer without progressing through the other two stages. Granted, some progress faster than others and for a variety of reasons.

If you understand and accept your current ability level, it will become easier to align your expectations with your ability. This may be one of the biggest steps toward improving the golf swing!

Description of Goals

Just as identifying skill level is important, it is important to identify goals. Some people simply enjoy hitting the ball out in the fresh air, and some people cannot enjoy anything unless it is done in a competitive atmosphere. In giving lessons I find it very important to understand why a person wants to play and what they expect to achieve. In fact I make the student fill out an information sheet and write down his or her goals as a golfer. Once we are on the same page, I can more effectively help that person move in the direction of their goal.

The following are four categories. You may fall into more than one category, and as your skill level improves, your goals may change.

No Specific Goal. This is a golfer who wants to strike the ball well enough to not embarrass him- or herself. Examples may be a wife who wants to play with her husband or a businessman who wants to entertain clients on a golf course.

Enjoyment. A golfer who wishes to swing well enough to hit some good shots and enjoy the time on the course.

Play Well. A golfer who is interested in score.

Competitive. A golfer who wants to have a consistent swing and develop his or her game to the fullest potential.

In a community college class I asked my students to fill out an information sheet. There were many retired people in these classes, including many very beginning older ladies. One such lady who didn't appear to have much of an athletic background wrote that she wanted to play in order to spend more time with her husband, who was an avid golfer. She got along very well in the class, and I felt like by the end of the semester she probably had achieved her goal. She came back a year later to take the course again, and her goal had changed. She said in bold writing that she wanted "to beat [her] husband's butt." So goals can change.

Limitations

If a golfer does not start the game as a very young person, certain limitations have a bearing on their ability to learn. Walt was a very poor student because he refused to consider any of his limitations.

These limitations can be overcome to an extent with careful and proper planning.

Time Constraint—How much time does it take to develop a credible game of golf? It varies depending on the individual, but for most of us it takes more than a small amount of time. Time factors that figure in the development of the golf swing are how much, when, and how long between practice sessions. The more often the practice and the less time between practice sessions, the better chance the golfer has to improve.

Athletic Background. Often we think of a good athletic background as being a benefit to playing golf. Sometime it is, but sometimes it is a hindrance. It is a help in the sense of coordination and timing, but it can be a detriment if the person takes a well-defined swinging pattern from one sport and it conflicts with the golf swing. Perception of power that has developed in another sport is another example of a difficulty to overcome. If the person has played a sport that requires strength to propel an object, they more than likely will take that same notion into the golf swing. How many really good golfers ever look like they use a lot of strength when they swing at a golf ball? "Swing easy" or "Let the club do the work" is good advice but may be next to impossible for the person who has the instincts to muscle it.

People who think of themselves as good athletes also tend to rate their ability a little too high. They expect to be as good in golf as they were in their other sport. This way of thinking usually holds the would-be golfer back.

A strong athletic background does not have to be a detriment; it can be an advantage. Hand-eye coordination, swinging patterns, ability to concentrate, and even experience in judging distances can be assets. These and other elements can speed up learning the game of golf if used wisely.

Physical Limitations. You should recognize any physical limitations and take them into consideration rather than ignore and try to develop a golf swing your body may not allow. For instance a person with a bad back is not going to swing like a young professional. Instead allowances must be made. This can be done, and the person with a bad back can learn to play the game very well.

An Oldie but Goodie. I received a phone call from a lady who complained that she was losing distance. I could tell over the phone that she was no spring chicken. Upon her arrival she informed me that she was eighty years old and didn't think she was going to win any long-drive championships but needed to hit the ball a little farther to keep up with "the girls." We worked together for several weeks on increasing the length of her backswing and she actually increased her distance a slight bit.

During the last lesson she told me she had a confession to make. She had lied about her age and was actually ninety, not eighty. Stunned, I asked why she had lied. Her answer was that she didn't want me to think she was too old to learn something different. She also explained that if I told any of her friends about her true age, I would be very sorry.

Unrealistic Expectations. I have already touched on this, and it is also dealt with in a later chapter. Golfers who want to improve must align their abilities with their expectations. This is one of the biggest faults that I find with people trying to learn. They try to perform at a level that is beyond their ability. As I mentioned earlier, good athletes are very prone to let this happen to them. Therefore you should identify your current skill level and try to improve to the next level.

Students have often commented on how patient I am. When I pass this on to my family, they usually have a good laugh. They don't see me as a very patient person, and in many endeavors I am not. In teaching golf it is different. Over the years I have developed an understanding of people and the way they learn. I usually can identify the level of the golfer and have a pretty good feel for how fast they can progress even at an early stage of our lessons. This helps me react to the student appropriately. So what is seen as patience is really just an understanding of learning.

Enjoy Learning the Game of Golf

There probably is no other sport quite like the game of golf. You can determine exactly how much you want to get out of your experience with the game. However, to reach your potential, be realistic. If you want to play as well as Tiger Woods, then you must have an incredible amount of natural ability as well as an abundance of time to practice. But most of all, enjoy, whatever happens. There are many worse things in life than a bad golf shot. And there surely are many things better than a good golf shot. But certainly the experience of a well-struck ball that travels high and far exactly as you intended is one of life's pleasures!!

Chapter

The Golf Shot

There are volumes written on golf equipment and the effect that it has on the golf shot. Companies tell you that their clubs, balls, and even shoes will absolutely give you a better golf shot than any other equipment that you could mistakenly purchase. This is regardless of your ability or golf swing. I will confess that over the years equipment has improved to the point where it certainly makes ball striking better. Still, a golfer cannot rely on equipment to learn the proper golf swing.

What really happens when the club strikes the ball? In this chapter we will look at the determining factors of the golf shot, the different flights the ball may take, and the progression of shots that might be expected from a beginner to an advanced player.

Mac Attack. Can a golfer not understand the mechanics of the golf swing, not care about equipment, and still develop a high level of feel for the underlying fundamentals of the golf swing? I met such a person years ago. His name was Mac and he was from my hometown.

He was a real live character in the way he talked, acted, and dressed. He owned perhaps the worst set of golf clubs known to man, and he couldn't make a putt if the hole was the size of a coffee can.

But the one thing Mac could do was hit a golf ball as well as anyone. He could hit it better than most tournament professionals, and he could do it with his crummy golf clubs. Over the years he had developed a tremendous feeling for the underlying fundamentals of the golf swing. I am sure he didn't know why the ball went where it did or even cared. It was as if the clubs were an extension of his body and he could control the movements perfectly. Parts of his swing looked a little peculiar, but in the important areas it must have been near perfect.

How good was Mac? This is one of the many stories that helped develop his legend. One summer day he showed up at the club for his weekly game. He occasionally had flare-ups of arthritis and his hands would swell up noticeably. This happened to be one of those days. He also pulled out his driver and displayed a club that was held together by a Band-Aid. As I mentioned earlier, his equipment was almost a part of his body, and when his driver hurt, it was as if he hurt as well.

His playing companions felt sorry for him, and in the course of arranging the customary bets they increased his handicap. Mac responded by shooting nine-hole scores of 31 and 32 for an eighteen-hole total of 63. He easily beat all of his opponents and won every bet.

It was shortly after this great round that Mac's driver shattered. It was as if part of Mac died that day, and he never played quite the same. I had the opportunity to play with Mac only once, and I was amazed at his ball-striking ability. He knew how to use his equipment and control the golf shot like only a few people I have ever observed.

Determining Factors

✳ **What are the determining factors?** They are the factors that dictate what happens to the golf ball. They determine where and how far the ball will travel. Regardless of how a golfer swings or what type of equipment he or she is using, success is difficult unless the determining factors are correct. The following are descriptions of these factors and references to the factors. Each determining factor has a distinct influence on the ball.

Ball Carry. How far the ball travels in the air.

Club Head Speed. Miles per hour of the golf club head at impact. Theoretically the faster the mph, the farther the ball will travel, but this depends on several factors.

Target Line. An imaginary straight line from the ball to the target. This is a point of reference when talking about the determining factors.

Club Face Angle. The direction the face of the club is pointing at impact in relation to the target. For a right-handed golfer *open* is to the right of the target and *closed* is to the left. *Square* is directly toward the target.

Club Path. The path that the head of the club travels during the swing in relation to the target line.

Inside Out	Travels from inside the target line to outside after impact.
Outside In	Travels from outside the target line before impact to inside after impact.

Inside to Inside	Travels from inside the target line before impact, on the target line at impact, and back to inside after impact.

Impact Point. The point on the face of the club where impact is made. The club face has three distinct impact points.

Toe	End of the club face farthest from the shaft
Center	Center of the club face
Heel	Point on the club face closest to the shaft

Tempo. The time that it takes from the start of the swing to impact.

Ball Flights

There are nine flights that an airborne golf ball can take. Although I have witnessed with my students over the years a number of unusual-looking shots, physics really determines what happens to a golf ball once it is in the air.

Every shot described below is in relation to the target line. Remember, that is the line that extends from the golf ball to the target. As in the rest of the book, each ball flight is from a right-handed golfer.

1. *Push slice* is a ball that starts to the right of the target and then curves right.

2. *Push* is a ball that has no curve but simply travels on a straight line to the right of the target.

3. *Push hook* is a ball that starts to the right and then curves back to the left.

4. *Slice* is a ball that starts straight, then curves right.

5. *Straight* is a shot that travels on a straight line. This shot needs true perfect backspin.

6. *Hook* is a ball that starts straight, then curves left.

7. *Pull slice* is a ball that starts left and then curves right.

8. *Pull* has no curve and travels simply straight to the left.

9. *Pull hook* is a ball that starts left and curves left.

Many things influence the flight. Moisture on the club and ball, mud, or the impact point on the face of the club all affect how the ball flies. The dimple pattern on the ball will make the ball go higher or lower, curve more or curve less. How soft or hard the ball is made will help add or subtract distance.

Years ago I worked at a driving range in which the teeing ground was blocked by the wind. About 180 yards off the tee, however, the wind would pick up as it swirled around the trees and buildings. I found that if I used an old range ball in which the dimple patterns were worn down, I could actually hit a ball that would start off with a hook, then, when it reached the wind, change into a slice. You could imagine the reactions I received from my students, especially when they were beginners and in large groups.

Shot Descriptions

The following are descriptions of golf shots, from bad to good.

Whiff. Missing the ball altogether. Beginners are good at this shot (or nonshot). Often it is so embarrassing that it will change the hopeful golfer's swing from a full stroke to one that simply makes contact with the ball.

Topped. Just catching a piece of the ball. Same mistake as a whiff, but results are better, giving the mistaken thought that the swing was better.

Slice. This is a ball that curves to the right. It is an easy shot to hit and takes only a bit more talent than a topped shot. Most golfers never get past this shot but only make compensations so they do not slice as much.

Thin. Thin shots are versions of a slice, but contact on the face of the club is not as solid. Not quite a topped shot but close. Contact with the ball is very low on the club face.

Fat. You don't get good results from this shot. As the name indicates, this is hitting the ground behind the ball. If this shot is properly interpreted, it can indicate improvement in the golf swing even though the results are poor.

Sky ball. This is from hitting the ball high on the club. The club moves underneath the ball, causing too much height and resulting in a loss of distance.

Hook. This is the opposite of the slice. For a right-hander the ball curves to the left. This shot is actually a good shot to practice because it helps develop the correct golf swing. To produce this shot takes an essential motion that a good swing requires.

High. The high shot is not the same as a sky ball in that it is usually a shot with more solid contact.

Draw. A ball that starts to the right of the target and gently hooks back. This shot is a requirement for golfers who want to become advanced players. The shot normally takes a good golf swing to accomplish. Once a person learns to draw the ball, then any shot is possible.

Fade. Often misinterpreted as a mini slice. The difference between this shot and a slice is that a fade requires good mechanics. The ball travels almost as far in the air as a draw. Better players use this type of shot because they do not need the distance that a draw will give and they like the control they receive with a fade.

Straight. This is the most difficult shot to hit, and the attempt often causes mechanical errors that lead to many poor shots. Everything must be perfect. Beginners often are obsessed with straight shots, and it holds back their development.

Chapter

Practice

I once heard a talk by a renowned golf instructor. Those of us in the audience found it very interesting when he said he did not let his students practice on their own. He explained that without supervision his students would not practice properly. In the ideal world that would be the perfect way for a person to learn the golf swing. But from a practical point it would be difficult to always have the instructor present.

Before we begin working on the golf swing, we should discuss practice. No matter who you are or how little time you have, there must still be some practice involved with learning the swing.

Where and How to Practice

Where can you practice? When I was first learning the game, it was much easier to practice. There was always an open field nearby where I could use my own golf balls. In those days golf courses usually set aside an area where you could bring your own golf balls to practice.

Although there were driving ranges, they were neither as abundant nor as popular as today. In the modern era of golf there is big money in practice, thus eliminating many of the free areas that we had in the past.

If you can find space where practice is permitted, that would be terrific. Usually in populated areas where land is at a premium it is very difficult to find that space. In fact I have seen signs that prohibit dogs, litter, and golfers. If that is the case where you live, then you need to find a driving range. Driving ranges can be either freestanding (away from a golf course) or at a golf course.

There is also practice that may be done in areas where hitting the ball is physically impossible. Perhaps you would like to practice at home without destroying the neighbors' property or on the road when you are stuck in a hotel room. I have tried to incorporate practice exercises that can be used without a golf ball and in some instances without a club.

What do you need? The driving range will provide the golf balls for a fee. If you don't have clubs, often the range will provide a club—just check with them beforehand. Wear comfortable clothes. Some places have a dress code. If the range has mats, golf shoes are not necessary; flat-soled shoes such as tennis shoes will certainly suffice.

Before you begin. Always start with some light stretching. After you have loosened up, take a few full swings without a ball. Depending on the type of practice plan you are working on (and we will discuss that in a few pages), hit a few easy short shots, then gradually work into a full swing. The type of practice will also determine the golf club that you will use. Generally in the initial stages of learning a lofted club such as a No. 7 iron will produce the best results.

How do you know if you are practicing properly? This is very difficult because usually the only source of feedback is the flight of the golf ball. Not many people are capable of analyzing the feedback properly, especially the beginner or intermediate golfer. Usually to them a good shot means a good swing and a poor shot means a poor swing, yet it could be just the opposite. At an early stage of learning luck plays a big part. This is probably why the instructor in the above illustration did not like his students practicing without his supervision. Often the golfer will give up on a good swing if it doesn't bring immediate results or keep using a poor swing if somehow it provides good shots.

For your practice to be effective you should have a plan before you begin. This plan should be very specific. Depending on the part of your swing you are working on, the golf shot may be in the form of a good shot, but it also may be in the form of something other than a good shot.

How often should you practice? My best students aren't necessarily the ones who practice the most. They usually are the ones who practice the most effectively. They all have a plan in mind and are very specific with the time they have available. I have to say that they do practice more than just once in a while. Make a regular scheduled practice time.

If you are taking lessons, I suggest that you practice at least twice between sessions. Make one of the times you practice shortly after you have taken the lesson. If you are not taking lessons, it is up to you how often you practice. Factors that influence your amount of practice may be how well you are playing and your goal as a golfer.

How long should you practice? I suggest you start with a small bucket or bag of balls. That way if the practice is not going well or fatigue sets in, you can simply stop. Often for economic reasons we buy a large quantity of balls, get tired or distracted, yet continue practicing because the balls are there and we don't want to waste the money.

What are practice drills? Shortly you will be introduced to the first of our practice drills. They are a very effective way to practice the golf swing. Each drill that is outlined in this book has a specific purpose. Many of the drills are a portion of the swing and will result in a portion of the shot. You should learn the drills in the proper sequence and what type of shot each drill will produce.

Can you practice too much? Probably if you are practicing the wrong things, even a little practice is too much. One student I had could be quite annoying. At the end of a particular lesson I told him to hit thirty buckets of balls before he returned. I was unaware that he had made an appointment that was to take place in three days. When he showed up for his next lesson, his left arm was visibly swollen, but he was very proud that he had hit thirty buckets of balls since I had last seen him. His arm hurt for about six weeks. In his case I would say that was entirely too much practice.

No matter what you are trying to achieve from your practice, enjoy the time. Treat it as a golf experience like playing. You will have good shots, bad shots, and in-between shots. You will be out in the fresh air and in an environment of fun. There are many worse places you could be spending your time.

Equipment

Obviously to play the game you need equipment. Clubs, golf balls, shoes—they are all important to the game. The equipment manufacturers may lead you to believe that the better the equipment and the more expensive it is, the better you will play. To play at a high level that may have some truth. But for what you need to accomplish, your goals are clubs that are the proper length and shaft flex, golf balls that will last, and shoes that are comfortable.

Equipment changes so fast that it is very difficult to keep up. The best bet for you is to go to a reputable pro shop and have a professional help you based on your goals, physical stature, and how much you would like to spend.

Golf clubs have changed dramatically over the years. Styles, shapes, and material all have an influence on the shots. But the purpose of the clubs is the same. You develop a golf swing, and when you have to hit the ball different distances, you change clubs, not the swing. You will notice with the iron clubs that the higher the number, the more loft or angle on the face of the club—thus a shorter shot and more height.

What type of clubs do you need? There are woods, irons and even clubs that are a combination of the two. Your ability level, experience, and expectations should dictate the clubs you need. A beginner really could get by with a basic set. The 3–9 irons, a pitching wedge, No. 3 wood, a No. 5 wood, and a putter would really get you started. As you progress, you will probably want to upgrade and fill in with other types of clubs.

For some people learning the golf swing can become a passion. For others, collecting golf equipment can be as much fun. I have seen my friend Stan, an equipment fanatic, purchase a putter at the end of nine holes before we started play on the back nine. When I questioned him about this, he asked, "Doesn't everybody?" I told him no, most people buy a hot dog.

How do I know the distance that each club will deliver? This is a question that I am asked frequently. Initially just getting the ball airborne may be good enough.

Eventually you will need to know how far each club will make the ball travel. With my students I suggest watching the No. 7 iron and judging how far the ball flies, then rolls. Once you think you are somewhat consistent with judging this distance, you can more or less add ten yards for a 6 iron, ten more for the 5, and so on, and subtract ten yards for the 8, ten more for the 9. This is not a precise formula but just a start for when you will need to go to the golf course and use the proper club.

Chapter

The Underlying Fundamentals of the Golf Swing

What are the underlying fundamentals? From my observations over the years these are the fundamentals that seem to be the foundation common with the best golfers. These same fundamentals are the ones that seem to be missing from almost all other golfers. We will call these three relaxation, club path, and hand action.

Why do people seem to improve only to a certain level and then the improvement stops? I truly believe that they have not developed the underlying fundamentals and that the foundation of their golf swing is based on compensations.

Why haven't these been recognized as the foundation of the golf swing? Only in recent years has instruction had the full benefit of videotape. Golf swings have been filmed for many years but not in a manner in which comparisons could be made between model swings and students' swings. It is in the comparisons between great, good, mediocre, and bad that you can see consistency in each level when it comes to certain parts of the swing.

In the mid-70s I was playing competitive golf on a regular basis. My game was at its best, and I had some moderate success in smaller tournaments. My vision like that of most aspiring golf professionals was to play on the PGA Tour.

The Illinois Open was a big event for me. The previous week I played in the qualifying round and had the low score of the day with a 68. I traveled to the site two days before the beginning of the tournament. The first practice round I played by myself, so only my caddie witnessed my round of 78. The second practice round I played with three other golf professionals who were good friends of mine and very good players. We had a spirited game and I shot an even par 72.

Because I had been the low qualifier, I was honored to play in the prestigious pairing of the day for the first round. This group included Jay Haas. Jay was just coming out of college and only a month earlier had tied for first at the NCAA Championship. He appeared to be destined for big things on the PGA Tour and has fulfilled that promise. This was one of his first tournaments as a pro, and the papers had duly noted his presence. I on the other hand was a seasoned professional with numerous tournaments under my belt and was determined to show Jay a shot or two. I did exactly that—actually I showed him 84 of them! It was an embarrassing and humiliating experience.

What happened? I had been playing well all summer, and to fold up in the most important round of the year and maybe of my life was very disappointing. That is the first topic of this chapter.

Relaxation

Is relaxation an underlying fundamental of the golf swing? My experience in the Illinois Open was a good example of relaxation being one of the underlying fundamentals. Entering the tournament I was swinging the club and hitting the ball extremely well. All three rounds then displayed my level of relaxation. In the first practice round I was too relaxed. During the second practice round I was very comfortable with my playing companions, which put me at the right level of relaxation. But during the third round I was so nervous, I could not relax. In my opinion relaxation may be the most important underlying fundamental of the golf swing!

What is relaxation? Being relaxed means the muscles are not tense and there is no feeling of nervousness or intimidation.

If a golfer is not relaxed, the golf swing will be inhibited and it becomes very difficult to create feel for the swing. Worse for the golfer who is attempting to learn or change the golf swing, development will be slowed.

It is a fact that a golfer must have a certain amount of tension to control his or her muscles. Too little tension, no control; too much tension, no control.

What is the right amount of tension? This varies with the individual and with the difficulty of the shot or situation, just as it did with me at the Illinois Open. The first practice round I was over-relaxed; my tension level was too low. The second round my tension was at the optimum level. I was playing with fellows who were friends and I was comfortable with the situation. The round with Jay Haas was obviously beyond my comfort level.

As the golf coach at Cal State University–Fullerton I observed this with very good golfers coming out of high school. They would have trouble shooting the same scores at the college level that they shot in high school. I see this all the time when I give playing lessons to my students. Rarely does a student play well the first time they play with me.

Why is relaxation important? The common error seems to be too much tension. Relaxation therefore becomes one of our most important underlying fundamentals of the golf swing. It is very difficult to perform, to improve, and to learn if a person is nervous or tense. And how could you possibly enjoy yourself under those circumstances? Even the simplest situation may frighten the beginner, providing too much tension.

How do golfers relax? It doesn't work to be told to relax. Playing partners cannot help the golfer relax. If the golfer concentrates too much on it, that won't work either. Most of the battle of conquering relaxation is confidence. If the golfer feels confident, he or she will be relaxed. But confidence is often hard to gather.

One thing you can try to do as a golfer is to forget the thousands of pieces of advice that you have heard. Trying to remember everything is just too complicated. Another thing is to keep your ability level in mind. It is hard to relax when expectations are beyond that level.

Accepting poor shots is another way to reduce tension. No golfer likes to hit poor shots, but unless you are skilled and experienced, then with few exceptions the percentage of poor shots over great shots is going to be higher. Every golfer should accept this and try to develop a golf swing that will allow the percentage of good shots to eventually outnumber the bad shots.

By creating a practice and playing atmosphere that takes into consideration the reasons for tension the golfer can learn to relax. By realizing that poor shots are part of learning, you can develop the golf swing by not trying to perform beyond your ability level but rather by attaining a particular level, then striving for the next. When this environment is produced, you have the opportunity to relax and learn.

The pig story. I grew up in rural Illinois. When I was first learning to play, I would hit balls in the fields near my home. Between the fields that I used for my practice was a pig lot. As hard as it is to believe, whenever my shots landed in their area, the pigs would eat my golf balls. Golf balls in those days were wound with rubber bands and filled with liquid centers. Apparently they tasted good, because the pigs gobbled them up faster than I could retrieve the things.

Whenever I showed up to practice, the pigs would suddenly appear for their golf ball snacks. Although the shot was less than 100 yards, having the pigs present put too much pressure on my developing golf swing. Pressure in golf may not be playing for thousands of dollars, but trying to hit your very last golf ball over a group of hungry pigs. Many days my practice ended early.

Years later I returned to my practice area and was amazed at how easy the shot looked. I didn't try a shot, but I am sure I would not have had any of the difficulty I experienced as a beginning golfer. The troubles I encountered in those early days were simply a case of low ability level and lack of confidence, leading to too much tension. Did this help me develop my swing faster? I am not sure, but my guess is no. It would have made my practice easier and my sessions would have lasted longer if I had become more proficient at that distance first without the pigs. Once my swing had developed, it would have been great practice.

How crucial is relaxation? You don't see many golf professionals with smooth-flowing swings who look nervous. In fact much of their pre-shot routine such as a waggle is done to rid tension from their body. At the end of a tournament when the shots mean the most is usually the only time you can tell that they are having trouble relaxing. When they are not able to overcome this tension, they are open to errant shots.

A good example may be Greg Norman in the 1986 Masters. He had played a tremendous game on the back nine, and one of the big factors was that Jack Nicklaus had taken all the attention away. Few people were paying attention to Norman simply because Nicklaus, who was playing ahead of him, played so fantastic. It wasn't until Norman was on the eighteenth hole that the pressure of the situation may have caught up with him. All he needed to do was make a par to tie and send the tournament into a playoff. Here was a person at the top of his game who all of a sudden may have become very nervous. This caused him to hold on to the club too tightly during his second shot. He hit the ball well right of the green, and his bogey 5 made him settle for second place.

If players of this magnitude need to be at the proper level of relaxation, it becomes even more critical for golfers who do not have the same ability—not only when they perform on the golf course but when they are learning the golf swing.

Relaxation Practice

How do you practice relaxation? This is a great starting point for you, especially if you are a new golfer. You can use this practice session for relaxation, as you develop you can use it for a warm-up routine, and as you progress in your game, you can use this session as a return to point if your swing runs into trouble.

We will start this practice session with a lofted golf club like a No. 7 iron. Before you begin swinging, do something to stretch your muscles. Twist with the club behind your back—anything except hard swings that might do you damage. Then make some slow swings without a golf ball. Nothing hard—just enough to loosen up.

Grip and stance are not as important at this stage as they will be later. I suggest holding the club loosely with both hands. If you are just beginning, hold the club similar to how you would hold a baseball bat with the exception that your thumbs point down the grip toward the club head. Your hands should be close together. Stand with both feet about as wide as your shoulders, and place the ball in the center of your stance and far enough away that your arms are straight but not stiff. Bend at the waist and bend your knees slightly. Your feet should be close to parallel with the target line. Too much emphasis on grip and stance will take away from the goal of this practice, which is to relax, move, and swing. I highly doubt that you will hit enough balls at this early stage to develop bad habits from a faulty grip or stance.

The objective of our first three drills is to develop rhythm and confidence, which leads to relaxation. If you think these drills are unnecessary or you already have a warm-up routine, please continue to the next underlying fundamental. In all three drills the accuracy or length of the shot is not important. Simply relaxed movement and striking the ball is the goal.

Drill 1—Short Swing Drill. Hold the club very lightly and take only swings in which the shaft of the club travels from waist high on the backswing to waist high on the follow-through. There is no target involved with this shot and the ball should travel only a short distance, thirty yards tops. You are simply trying to make contact. If you need to put the ball on a tee, it is permissible in this drill. One tip is to make contact with the ground and the ball at the same time. That motion will make the ball travel in the air, not trying to lift or help it up. This shot is called a *pitch shot* and is one we will use later in the short game chapter.

Drill 2—Three-Ball Drill. Line up three balls in a row about three inches apart. Stand two feet away from the closest ball and begin swinging continuous practice strokes the same length as in Drill 1. As you develop a little rhythm and control, begin walking forward and without stopping the swing, strike each ball one after another.

Warning: As you first attempt this drill make sure no one is standing directly behind you, because there is no guarantee that the balls will go forward. This is a great drill because it requires movement, reaction (not much time to think), and rhythm.

Drill 3—Full Swing Drill. In this swing, again there is no target. It is one in which you may have to use your best Tiger Woods imitation. Simply make a full, long backswing and a full, long follow-through. Often beginners in their attempt to just make contact with the ball shorten and tighten up the swing. In light of that even if you miss the ball altogether it is okay as long as you complete the swing.

My stock response to students who have difficulty hitting the ball and let it bother them is to say, "What do you expect? You are not very good." I continue on and explain that the golf swing is a very complex movement and that without much experience, contact on a full swing is difficult. But with practice and developing form you will become more and more consistent.

I make sure I give the follow-up answer very quickly. I don't mean to insult anyone but have found that it is a great way to lower expectations and make a person relax. One time, though, I taught a young lady who was very insulted by my remark. Before I could apologize, she had stormed away.

Practice Routine—the Nine Ball. Once you have attempted the three drills, put them together into a routine such as this. If you are on a driving range, take all nine off to the side so that you can keep track of where you are in the routine. The first three balls are the Short Swing Drill, the next three are the Three-Ball Drill, and the final three are the Full Swing Drill.

If you are just starting out, keep repeating the sequence for the entire practice. Later as you move on in your development this will become your warm-up routine. In future practice sessions it may be used as a practice to start over and regain confidence or rhythm. Remember, these are relaxation exercises, and often even better players find tension a big fault in the swing.

Club Path

"Stubby" was a good friend of mine and one of those real life characters. We worked at the same golf course and played many rounds of golf together. He was a former college baseball player who had plenty of power, and with his nickname you could imagine what he looked like. The big problem with Stubby's golf game was his incredible slice. In order to hit the ball in the fairway he often had to allow forty to fifty yards of curve.

His slice was legendary in west central Illinois. It was hilarious when on rare occasion he would line up way to the left and the ball would go straight. Sometimes it was pure agony to watch him try to play a dogleg left or any hole that had obstacles on the left side of the fairway.

It seemed as though Stubby tried every cure known to man to correct his slice. Some would work temporarily, but all ended up with the same result: at least the same amount of slice if not more.

The problem was his club path. It was always outside in, and every correction he tried would be a compensation for the club path. Never in all the time that I played golf with Stubby did he practice to correct his swing. The practice was always directed toward the golf shot.

What is club path? The term *club path* describes the path that the head of the club travels during the swing. There are three paths that the club may take: *Inside out* means the head of the club travels on a path that moves from inside the target line on the backswing to outside the target line after impact. *Outside in* is a club head that is moving from outside the target line on the downswing to inside after impact. This is the easiest, most common natural route that a person may swing on, but it is the one that creates most bad shots. *Inside to inside* is a path in which the club head moves from inside the target line to square at impact to inside after impact.

If a person is using a putter, the club could also move straight back and straight through the target line. The reason is the putter is the straightest of all the clubs and is the one that is most capable of traveling straight. That is a good thing when you need accuracy but not distance.

A good way to understand club path is to sit at a driving range for a time and watch people swing. After a short time you will see how the struggling golfers pull their arms and the club across their bodies, generally imparting a slice spin on the ball.

Why is club path important? For most golfers the desired result of the shot is to get the ball near the target. The flight of the ball is determined by three factors: the angle of the club face at impact, the path that the club head has taken during the course of the swing, and the speed of the club head.

The angle of the club face in relation to the target at impact determines the direction of the ball, and the speed of the club head determines distance, but both are dictated by the club path.

What is the correct club path? Depending on the type of ball flight the golfer desires, the club path differs. For the student trying to develop a golf swing the best club path is inside out. This club path will help the golfer feel the correct golf swing and have a ball flight that is right to left or a draw for a right-handed player.

Many golfers make the mistake of letting the target influence the club path. In their desire to hit the ball straight toward the target they rarely swing the club the way it is designed. Actually many golfers attempt to swing a golf club as if it were a putter, straight away from the target and straight back to the target. Usually the golfer who attempts to swing this way ends up swinging outside in. Although it is the most natural and the easiest way to swing a club, it almost never results in a squarely struck golf shot. The typical results are slices, pull-hooks, or topped shots.

Even as long ago as the 1940s Percy Boomer described the error in his book *On Learning Golf*. He called it Golf Bogey Number 1: "The natural inclination to achieve the desired result." I am sure he was talking about golf, but he may have been making a parallel to life as well.

The Brothers. I was writing a paper for a class in motor development. The paper was on the influence of the target in developing a skill movement. At the time I was writing the paper I happened to be giving lessons to brothers ages eight and twelve. The eight-year-old had little experience in anything, but his older brother had played Little League and several other sports. He knew what a target was, and he knew what it took to make a ball travel distance.

The eight-year-old immediately developed an excellent golf swing. His target was the golf ball and nothing else. His swing looked like one you would see in a magazine. The twelve-year-old had a much more difficult time. His swing was very adult-like. His shoulders moved around too quickly and his club path was outside in. The target had a definite influence on his swing.

What does the proper club path feel like? Club path is a widely misunderstood feeling of the golf swing. What appears to happen during the stroke and what actually occur are generally different. This is because of the speed of the swing, the momentum of the body, the centrifugal force of the club head, and the lag time of the sensation of contact.

I have read several publications that say the golf ball has traveled approximately fifteen feet before the golfer ever senses contact. In other words the golfer is not in the position of the swing that he or she believes or feels that they are in at the time. Their sensations are always behind their actual physical position. Therefore as a golfer tries to swing straight toward the target they will invariably end up swinging to the left. This is because of the fact that they are not at the point of the swing they feel and the momentum of the body is pulling left.

The Broken Club. During a lesson one afternoon this reaction-time idea was proved to me. I was taping a gentleman's golf swing from the side view. In the course of his full swing with a 7 iron the head of his club broke off. When we played the shot back on the video, we could actually see the ball leave and the club head flying behind. Most amazing was the expression on his face. It changed dramatically when he was about halfway into the follow-through, or when the ball was about fifteen feet away from the original position.

Club path is an underlying fundamental. You can have a beautiful-looking, smooth swing, but if your club is not traveling in the proper direction, your swing into the impact area must compensate for it.

The High Jumper. One of the best illustrations that I have seen of a faulty club path happened one day at a local golf course. A member of our group was sick, and the starter put in a fellow who happened to be a world-class high jumper. His golf swing showed his athletic ability. It was smooth and flowing, but his club path was outside in, and he sliced every shot. This cost him distance and was very perplexing for a person who obviously was highly physically skilled.

Club Path Practice

The drills in this section will help you develop the feel for the proper swing. This will be done by using the flight of the ball. In other words we will control the Knowledge of Results to train us in proper club path. Remember, often the feelings of the swing are different than the look of the swing.

This is also a good time to work on your setup or stance. A square stance is best for all of our practice drills. A square stance includes not only your feet but also your hips and shoulders. All three should be on a line parallel to the target line. To achieve this position the left shoulder (for a right-hander) should feel like it is slightly elevated. The reason for this is that the right hand extends farther down the grip of the club than the left hand.

I believe how far you stand from the ball is individual. Much depends on your body structure. I would avoid bending over too much or standing too straight from the waist. Your knees should be slightly bent. Your arms should be straight but not stiff. The person who stands close to the ball will have an upright or vertical swing. The person who stands farther from the ball will have a flat or horizontal swing. Your address is usually dictated by your height, your arm length, and the club you are using.

The ball should be placed just left of center when using the iron clubs and off the left instep with the woods. As you progress in the game, this may vary with different shots and in different situations. But at this time we are trying to simplify and make this as basic as possible. There are volumes written on the stance. It might be a good idea to pick up a magazine and select a golfer who fits your body type. Emulate his or her setup. Even if you have only a little knowledge of the golf swing, you can look in a mirror and tell whether you are standing correctly. Your stance will develop as you practice the following exercises, but by looking at your reflection you can practice this aspect without going to the driving range.

Drill 4—Push Drill. This is the foundation of the golf swing. When you achieve the feeling for this exercise, you will have developed a part of the swing to build on. We will use the flight of the ball to train your arms in the proper motion. The ball flight will not be straight toward the target but actually at an angle to the right of the target line.

Select a target and take a square stance by using a mat or lay a club across your feet—anything that is parallel to the target line. The swing in this drill is a partial backswing. The clubs and your arms travel in and away from the target line. At the end of this short backswing your club should be around waist high and your hands will be just off your right hip, neither forward nor behind. On the downswing the club head is traveling toward the ball at an angle inside the target line, not straight. At the end of this partial swing your arms and club shaft should point to the right of the target about 30 degrees and should be no higher than your waist. The ball flight should be on a direct line and travel only about thirty yards in the same direction as the club and your arms. If you are having trouble making yourself stop at the proper position, then you are putting more power into your swing than necessary.

If this were a baseball diamond, your ultimate goal would be centerfield, which is where you are aligned. But in this shot you are swinging toward right field. The ball should travel only as far as the distance of first base or about thirty yards.

Drill 5—Long Push Drill. This is the same idea as the Push Drill, but now you should make a full relaxed swing. Ideally the ball will actually go straight in the direction the feet, hips, and shoulders are aligned. Occasionally this happens during my lessons. If it does, it usually is with students under the age of nine. For some reason young kids can just let it go. As we grow older, it is more difficult to just let the club swing, so don't be surprised if this ball continues to go to right field.

Practice Routine. After you have warmed up properly using the nine-ball routine or your own routine, take three balls and lay them off to the side. With ball one and two perform the Push Drill. With ball three try the Long Push Drill. Results may be either good or bad but not as important as the results of the Push Drill.

Warning: Fat shots (hitting behind the ball) could be result from this practice. They are not necessarily the results of a bad swing but from the lack of timing. Your club more than likely is approaching the ball from a different angle, and until you learn to time the release properly, you may make contact with the ground first. This is a case where a poor shot is not necessarily a bad sign.

Home Practice. In the backyard you may try this without a ball. Put a soft barrier on the left side of your follow-through. If you don't swing on the proper path, you will hit the barrier. As you become proficient, move the barrier closer to the target line. Make sure you use something soft so that you don't break a club. With one student I suggested a plastic garbage can. She asked me if she could use her husband, Charlie, instead, because she didn't want to ruin a good garbage can. I told her okay.

Reminder: If you are having problems and get frustrated, you can always return to the relaxation lesson.

Hand Action

Are you a member of the famed Chicken Wing Society? That is the name one of my students gave to all golfers who bend their left elbow immediately after impact, forming the appearance of a chicken wing. A high percentage of golfers make this movement, and although it allows them to compensate and have a chance to hit a reasonably straight shot, it robs them of any true distance. Accuracy and consistency also are very hard to come by.

What is hand action? This may not be the appropriate term because we are describing more the motion of the arms before, during, and after impact. Golfers have used various terms and phrases in talking about this motion. *Snap the wrists, roll the wrists, cross the arms, pronation, supination,* and the *release* have all been used to help people produce this movement. Whatever and however you want to describe it is fine.

Occasionally I get some argument that this motion does not happen during the golf swing. My answer is to find me a picture in a magazine or book of a good golfer who does not have their forearms crossed over after contact with the ball. I had never seen that picture until one day a student brought me one of a famous person. This former major-league ballplayer actually hit the ball quite well and far with a chicken-wing finish. Of course he was a very strong and talented athlete, which most of my students are not. Occasionally I would see his name in pro tournaments and he almost always finished last. I just wonder how good he may have become if he had had the proper swing.

Why is hand action important? Distance comes from the speed of the club head at impact. To obtain maximum club head speed, the hands and arms must be used effectively. Accuracy is squaring the club face at impact. It can be done without proper hand action, but then the golfer must make compensations and use their body too much.

How are the hands and arms used properly? As the downswing is made, the hands and arms should naturally rotate to the left, or counterclockwise for a right-hander. This turning motion or rotation starts before contact with the ball and continues after contact. This is a very natural movement and is almost instinctive in other sports. An example is the throwing motion.

How do you understand the feeling of hand action? Similar to the club path the golfer is never in the position that they feel they are in. If they attempt to release or turn their hands and arms when they feel contact, the ball will already be in flight.

Is the grip important in hand action? The grip plays an important part in the ability to use your hands and arms properly. Often we burden golfers by showing them and making them hold the golf club perfectly. I believe like the setup that a grip can be learned more effectively as the swing is being learned. In other words the grip has to be learned, not shown. A perfect grip from the outset often gives golfers a weak feeling and they tend to use other movements to compensate for it.

You see a variety of grips. With most grips the golfer must make some form of compensation in his or her swing. That is why I like to develop a shot first that does not need compensation and makes it easier to hold the golf club properly. The three grip positions are neutral, weak, and strong. The names refer to the position that the hands have on the grip of the club. In the neutral grip the back of the left hand and palm of the right hand are parallel to the target line. In a weak grip the hands are turned to the left, and in a strong grip they are turned to the right. In the first drill of this practice it is difficult to have much success with anything that is not close to the neutral grip.

Place the club on the ground with the face of the club pointing toward the target. With the left hand put the club diagonally across the fingers with the grip under the heal pad. The left thumb should be slightly on the right side of the club. Leave a short gap between your hand and the end of the club. In the right hand again place the club diagonally across the fingers. Your hand should be placed over the left thumb and the right thumb should be slightly on the left side of the grip.

As you look straight down at the head of the club, you will have common checkpoints in the grip that have been used for years. In the left hand you should be able to see the first two knuckles. Any more and the grip is too strong; any less and the grip is too weak. In the right hand you should have a V formed with the thumb and forefinger. This V should point between your right shoulder and head. Too far to the right and it is strong; too far to the left and it is too weak. The easy and most comfortable mistake is the strong grip.

There are three ways to bond your hands onto the club: the baseball, the interlocking, and the overlapping grip. The purpose of each is to allow your hands and arms to work together. I suggest that a person start with a baseball, progress to the interlocking, and, if they are comfortable, end up with the overlapping grip. Much depends on the individual's hand size. Tiny, weak hands may want to use the baseball, small hands the overlapping, and medium and up the overlapping. Don't get hung up on any certain type of grip. Most good players use the overlap, but Jack Nicklaus and Tiger Woods both use the interlock and they have done fairly well.

Probably the best advice I can give you on the grip is in regard to how tightly you hold the club. Most people hold the club much too tightly, making it difficult to allow the hands and arms to rotate properly.

Hand Action Practice

Drill 6—The Hook Drill. This ball is going to hook or curve way to the left for a right-handed golfer. Line up in a square stance and with a neutral grip. Make a long backswing. On the downswing do whatever it takes—too soon of a release, too early, too much—but make the ball hook an extreme amount. How do you do it? Your right arm must cross over your left very early, even before contact with the golf ball. This may seem like an oddball shot, but it will develop the necessary motion that is required in a proper golf swing. By doing this you certainly can feel the motion. Visualize the face of the club hitting the outside portion of the ball, not directly behind the ball.

Practice Routine. Take three balls. Ball one and ball two are the Hook Drill. With ball three use our full relaxation swing and see what happens. Evaluate the shot on whether you used too much hand action or not enough.

Home Practice. Take a weighted club of some type. There are several on the market. A special club call the Swing Assist is very good. Make full practice swings, letting the club do the work. Feel the crossover of the arms as it occurs.

Combination Practice

To this point we have three types of practice: relaxation, club path, and hand action. Now it is time to combine the three in one practice session.

The Nine Ball. Use this routine from the relaxation section as a warm-up. Put nine balls off to the side. With the first three make short easy swings. The second three are in a row, and the final three are full swing. Remember, in this exercise straight and powerful are not the objective. Relaxation, contact, and rhythm are what you are trying to achieve. Once you feel comfortable, move on to the next set of drills.

Drill 7—The Combination Drill. To perform this drill you make a full swing combining the Push Drill and the Hook Drill. Ideally the ball will start to the right of the target and draw.

Practice Routine. Use three balls. Use ball one for the Push Drill, ball two for the Hook Drill, and finally, with ball three put everything together into the Combination Drill. With balls one and two focus on the mechanics during the shot. With ball three try to combine the two and analyze after the shot what happened. The shot was either a correct combination of the two drills or it was the lack of one or the other, in some cases lack of both. For example, a pull hook would mean there was not enough of the motion of the Push Drill, a push would indicate the lack of the Hook Drill, and a slice would indicate the lack of both.

This is a simple way to analyze your golf swing, not only on the driving range but on the golf course as well. A good shot is the correct combination of the two drills. A bad shot shows a lack of one of the two or maybe both. It rarely would be overdoing either movement!

Initially this may seem like a very complex and complicated way to swing the golf club. But as you progress as a golfer, it is very important, especially when you begin using longer clubs. It has been my experience that once you become proficient at the push and hook drills, it is much easier to combine the two. Therefore put more importance on those two drills individually than on the combination.

Chapter

Form

I was practicing at a local driving range one afternoon. It was very crowded, and golfers were whacking balls out right and left with one exception. A young man was standing near the pro shop window watching the reflection of his backswing. He would swing the club to the top of the backswing, then stop and look. He then would turn around to the other direction and view that angle. He practiced this for a long time. I wonder who benefited the most from their practice that day, the people banging out balls or the young man working on the form of his swing.

Backswing

Not many golfers who are attempting to learn the game of golf take the time to develop the feeling for the arms, hands, and club head on the backswing. For the most part their practice is full bore, straight-ahead golf shots. Once the club leaves their field of vision, it is not only out of sight but out of mind, touch, and feel. It only makes sense that a golfer who wants to be consistent on the downswing should have control enough to be consistent on the backswing.

What is the backswing? Any skill movement has three phases: preparation, force, and follow-through. In golf the backswing is the preparation phase. In other words the golfer is preparing to put the power in the downswing or force phase. The backswing begins with the initial movement of the club away from the ball and ends when the movement starts toward the ball. Keep in mind that there are times when different body parts are in different phases of the swing at the same time.

Why is the backswing important? The backswing often becomes so complicated that the force phase, or downswing, becomes little more than a correction. Because the downswing happens very quickly, there is not enough time to completely correct errors made in the backswing. This leads to mis-hits, lack of speed, and many other errors. Often a poor golf shot is a direct result of a faulty backswing.

Professional or good amateur players for the most part have simple backswings that require little energy and expend little force. The novice or intermediate in contrast will typically waste energy with a fast and complex motion that leaves a dissipating, if any true, force for the downswing.

What is swing plane? *Swing plane* describes the relationship your body, your arms, and the club shaft have with the ground and to the ball. Flat is too horizontal; upright is too vertical. A flat swing promotes a hook, and an upright swing promotes a slice.

How is a good backswing performed? A good backswing consists of a simple movement that does not extend too far back or stop too short. It doesn't have to be real slow, but in all of my years I have never heard anyone say that their backswing was too slow; rather they say just the opposite. The plane of the swing should not be flat or upright. It should match your body size and address position.

Of all the parts of the golf swing to describe, the backswing is the most difficult. Even a crystal-clear description is not always interpreted correctly. The fact of the matter is that you are trying to perform a movement that is to control an implement preparing to strike an object. And you are doing this out of your field of vision. You may as well be blindfolded—which doesn't work, by the way.

In my description there are two parts to the backswing: the takeaway and the body rotation. The takeaway starts with the hands and arms. It is the initial motion of the backswing. It takes place roughly between the ground and the waist. It requires very minimal movement with the body. Since the hands and arms are the body parts that are capable of moving the fastest, they may be best controlled by early use rather than late use. This can be an argumentative description of the motion. When I first learned to play the game, the saying was to keep the club as low and as straight back as possible. This made for a very loose finish at the end of the backswing, because I cocked my wrists at that point. Over the years the golf swing has evolved into cocking the wrists or setting the hands at an earlier stage in the swing.

The common mistake that I have seen in the backswing is rotating the body too early. When this occurs, the golfer will either compensate with a wristy motion at the top of the swing or take too short of a backswing. The result is loss of club control with a long swing and a loss of power with a short swing.

Remember on the takeaway the head of the club does not travel straight back but comes inside the target line. When the club has reached parallel with the ground, approximately waist high, it should also be parallel with the target line. At this point your hands should be in line with your right hip. The back of the left hand should be facing straight away or close to parallel with the target line, not toward the sky or toward the ground.

After a proper takeaway in which the body has remained relatively stationary, the rotation begins. The torso starts turning clockwise (right-hander) once the club is around hip level. The torso and left knee should then rotate inward. The left foot should also rotate inward, which may allow it to come off the ground slightly to enable this movement to take place. Allow this to happen naturally—don't force it. Once the body cannot rotate any farther, the backswing should stop. There should be no play in the hands, arms, and club at the end of the backswing. If the takeaway has been made properly, this stable position will occur. The club may or may not be parallel to the ground. It depends on your body flexibility and the club you are using. More important is that the club shaft is not too flat, horizontal, nor too upright, vertical. If at the end of the backswing you were to let loose of the club so it dropped, it would not hit you in the head but land slightly above your shoulder.

At the end of the backswing your back doesn't necessarily have to point toward the target, and your left shoulder doesn't have to point toward the ball. You simply need to twist, turn, rotate (whatever description you like) as much as you are capable without losing control of the club. It has often been said that the club and body turn in one movement. This perception of the backswing often results in a very fast motion and is not wrong, but it takes quite a lot of practice to develop the timing to control the swing in this manner.

The backswing is difficult to learn and extremely difficult to change. It can be done, but it takes patience on the part of the golfer, many swings without a golf ball, and some form of visual feedback. As I mentioned above, a large part of the problem certainly lies in the fact that you cannot see yourself during the backswing. This leads to relying on the golf shot for feedback, and when you are practicing the backswing, the resulting shot is not the most accurate source.

Don't Be Like Mike. Mike was a great guy who had an extremely difficult time with the backswing. His swing was very flat or horizontal. I could help him by holding his club in the proper position at the top of the backswing, and when I let go, he actually could hit the ball quite nicely. But left on his own it would take only a few seconds to slip back to his flat ways.

One day Mike brought his own videotape for me to use and for him to watch at home. He was away for a minute, so I put the tape in the machine to make sure it was at the correct spot. He had accidentally rewound the tape to a part that showed him practicing on his own. The practice wasn't on the driving range, it was in his living room late at night and he was wearing his pajamas. His backswing was actually very good because he had to avoid hitting the sofa.

Mike was quite embarrassed that I had seen him in his pajamas, but watching the tape of his practice helped during the lesson. The backswing he was making in the tape was the best I had seen him do on his own. He told me that to miss the couch he felt like his club moved away from his body and actually felt like it was on top of his head at the end of the backswing. As our lesson unfolded that day, his backswing improved with those two key thoughts. This made it very difficult for him to hit the golf ball initially, but with a lot of practice he was able to overcome his ugly backswing. I hope he threw away the pajamas as well, because they were the only things that made his backswing look good.

Backswing Practice

The purpose of this practice is to help you develop feeling for the backswing. As I mentioned earlier, most people tend to overlook the backswing, but it is highly critical to one's ability to be consistent on the downswing.

Drill 8—Takeaway Drill. From a square stance take the club waist high and stop. Stop for a good second or two. Look into a mirror or window, or have someone watch you. If the club has traveled too far, start over again. The club should be parallel to the ground and also to the target line. If it is at the right height, focus back to the ball and slowly swing forward, making contact. You can create the takeaway by cocking your wrists or by moving your arms, but there should be very minimal body movement.

Drill 9—Backswing Completion Drill. From a square stance take the club waist high and come to a complete stop. Then finish the backswing by slowly rotating your body. When your body quits turning. stop swinging. The club should be in a very controlled position. Once you have held this position for a second or two, make a nice, slow, relaxed downswing, hitting the ball only a short distance.

This drill has very little momentum, so the club will not travel back as far as it will during a normal-pace swing. Again get into a position where you can see yourself or have someone watch you. If you make a mistake, start over.

Routine. Use three balls. Use ball one for the Takeaway Drill and ball two for the Completion Drill. With ball three return to the Combination Drill from the previous practice. Try to make the ball start to the right and draw back. The backswing is the main concern with this practice. The golf shots are not the priority, so the results may not be great.

Home Practice. Same practice as above but without a ball and using a mirror or some other form of visual feedback.

Downswing

In the early and mid-70s I played many tournaments in Florida. One day instead of playing I attended the PGA Citrus Open near Orlando and followed Gene Littler for the entire day. His nickname on tour was Gene the Machine. It was easy to see why he had earned that name. I was amazed at his effortless swing and the power he achieved from it.

His backswing was slow and smooth, which many people can attain, but the unforgettable part was that his downswing was also slow and smooth. Although he showed very little force, the ball always traveled a great distance. How he attained that force is the next topic of this chapter.

What is the downswing? The downswing is the force phase of the golf swing. It occurs once the backswing is completed. It is the one part of the golf swing that is fast and powerful. The purpose of the downswing is to deliver the face of the club squarely to the ball with as much speed as possible. The oft-repeated terms *over the top, spinning out,* and *casting* all describe mistakes in the downswing.

Why is the downswing important? The downswing influences the angle and speed of the club head at impact. The transition from the backswing to the downswing is not only a difficult movement but is the motion most prone to error for golfers of all levels. Once initiated, the downswing takes a fraction of a second, so there is little chance for recovery from backswing or initial downswing mistakes.

How is the downswing performed? There are numerous descriptions of the initiation of the downswing. Many golfers initiate the downswing by turning the upper body too early. The downswing, instead, begins with a movement of the lower body. The movement tends to vary with the individual. It could be a shift of the left hip or the knees moving in the direction of the target. The precise movement is the one that works for the individual. The general movement is the weight shifting from the back foot to the forward foot before the club, arms, and hands begin the forward movement.

In better players we often see a pause at the end of the backswing. This pause is actually the transition from backswing to downswing. At this phase the arms are not moving at all but the lower body has begun the downswing. Many very fine golfers have swings that appear different, even erratic. Yet all of these golfers have common traits in their downswing. The club head approach to the ball, weight shift, and release are very similar.

One of the best golf swings I have seen was from a fellow who was not a golfer at all but a world-class fast-pitch softball pitcher. I actually videotaped his pitching motion, and in the course of this he hit a few golf shots. Apparently the motions for both pitching a softball and hitting a golf ball are similar, because he had all the makings of a tremendous golfer.

When and how much leg motion is in the downswing has always been a point of controversy with golf instructors. My observation is that most beginning to intermediate players use their legs too little. Occasionally I find a person who overuses his or her legs on the downswing, but they are almost always the advanced players.

An Interesting Study. A few years ago a very well-known golf publication printed an article on what they believed was a revelation in golf instruction. In their study they had several tournament professionals hit shots while standing with each leg on a platform scale. They took pictures of their swing and the scale in the background. It was noted that the scale showed that most of the weight was still on the back leg at impact. This was consistent with each player. The magazine suggested that the legs really did not initiate the downswing and concluded that perhaps golf instructors had been teaching incorrectly for many years.

Shortly after the article was published, I attended a PGA teaching conference. One of the speakers talked about the article. He actually went a step further. He had videotaped himself using the same type of scale. He did not hit a golf shot but instead crouched down in a position to jump straight up. Over his shoulder you could see that he weighed 185 pounds. He then jumped up in the air. As he was at the peak of the jump, the scale was visible and he still weighed 185 pounds. It wasn't until he began his descent that the scale moved. The one factor that the magazine article forgot to take into consideration was that the scale had a time lag.

The conclusion I came to from this presentation was twofold. One, I still believe that most of the weight has shifted to the front foot at impact, and two, magazines will publish anything.

Downswing Practice

This is the toughest practice session of all because it happens in a very short time frame. Shots are usually not good, because the drills are very mechanical and require much thought.

Drill 10—One-Leg Drill. Stand on your left leg and drop your right leg behind you, similar to a pelican. Make a short backswing and follow through working on your balance. This is a very good drill to help you let the club do the work.

Drill 11—Short Downswing. From a square stance take a short backswing and stop the club about waist high. Start the forward movement by shifting your weight in an exaggerated fashion.

Opening the hips, moving your right knee and right foot inward or toward the target. Once you have completely shifted your weight, let your arms move forward and strike the ball. The key to this drill is that your club should not move until you have shifted your weight! This is a very difficult and awkward drill but a crucial one. If you have trouble with this exercise, you are probably swinging too soon with your upper body. The follow-through should be short, about the same length as the backswing. During this drill you could say to yourself, "Stop, shift, and swing." Make a two-second interval between shift and swing.

Routine. Use three balls for this routine. With the first ball do the One-Leg Drill. Use ball two for the Short Downswing, and use ball three for the Combination Drill. Remember, the purpose of this practice is to develop weight shift. It is very difficult to work on this and have good timing. Until you develop proper timing, often the resulting shots are push slices, so don't be surprised if that happens to you.

Home Practice. Extend your left arm and hold on to something, such as a desk or a table. Take your right arm away as if making a backswing. Shift your weight forward, then swing your right arm, all the time not letting your left arm bend or move. Occasionally you see a tour player doing this on television using the shaft of the golf club sticking straight up from the ground.

Follow-Through

My one and only opportunity to play Pebble Beach was a great experience. The eighth hole was especially significant for a couple of reasons. First, it is one of the great golf holes in the world, and second was the manner in which I played the hole.

Having never played the golf course I used the wrong club on several occasions and particularly off the tee on number eight. I hit a driver and actually pushed the ball slightly. It came to rest within a few feet of the hazard. Now, on some golf courses the hazards are not very well defined, but on this particular hole it is very clear cut. It is a sheer drop-off—I'm not sure how many feet, but it goes straight down a long way. Looking over the edge I got that queasy, dizzy feeling you get from being on a high building.

The problem this posed was that unless I wanted to take a penalty, I had to hit the shot from this precarious position. The people I was playing with were highly competitive, so it left me with little choice. How much does the follow-through affect the golf shot? I made several practice swings with no problem, but when I made my actual swing at the ball, I thought the follow-through would carry me over the edge. This caused me to abruptly stop my swing, fall back on my right foot, and hit a line drive that traveled well over the green—and on number eight, that is not the place to be.

Does the follow-through affect your golf swing? Absolutely. Just put something in your way that inhibits the completion of the follow-through and see if it doesn't change the rest of your swing.

What is the follow-through? It is the final phase of any movement. It is the completion of the stroke and if left uninhibited will reveal what has occurred in the force phase.

Like the backswing the follow-through can be seen with the naked eye. It is the point in the swing where all parts are slowing down. The follow-through should be a reflection of the downswing. In other words a good downswing should create a good follow-through, a bad downswing a bad follow-thorough. That is not always the case. Much of the time you can interpret mistakes in the swing by looking at the follow-through, but sometimes a person can learn to adapt around the faults.

What should the follow-through look like? After impact with the ball both arms extend. The right arm crosses over the left as the club travels from impact to waist high. As the entire motion begins slowing down, the arms begin to fold. The hands and forearms should end up over the left shoulder. The weight should be completely shifted to the left side. The hips should be facing the target, and the heel of the back foot should be facing straight back.

Is the follow-through the same for everyone? Obviously everyone is different, so every follow-through will be different. It also depends on the type of shot the person is trying to execute. A draw will produce a flatter, more horizontal follow-through and a fade will give the golfer a more upright or vertical follow-through.

Can you use the follow-through to change your swing? Although the follow-through is a reflection of the downswing, trying to make a nice finish will certainly have positive results on your golf swing. Just because a golfer has a nice follow-through does not mean they have a nice swing. But it certainly can't hurt to have a nice, stylish, balanced follow-through.

A complete follow-through would be the main reason a good golf instructor would not tell a student to keep his or her head down. Keeping your head down does not allow the motion that is necessary to finish the swing thoroughly.

Follow-Through Practice

Drill 12—Short Follow-Through and Return. In this drill you start the swing in an abrupt follow-through position rather than a normal address. This is not a complete follow-through but one that is waist high with the club shaft pointing to the right of the target, with arms extended, crossed over, and weight shifted. From this position take a short backswing, then return to the follow-through. The goal of the drill is to return to the starting position. The ball just happens to be in the way of the swing. It is a little tricky because you have to miss the ball on the backswing, but with a little practice it can be done. If you swing too hard, it will be impossible to stop the club in the correct position.

Drill 13—Full Follow-Through and Return. This is similar to Drill 12 except in this exercise you start from a full follow-through position instead of a normal address. From the full follow-through take a complete backswing and then return to the full follow-through position. The goal is to complete the follow-through. Again you need to avoid the ball on the backswing portion.

Routine. Use three balls. With ball one perform the Short Follow-Through and Return Drill. With ball two practice the Full Follow-Through and Return Drill. Use ball three for the Combination Drill.

Full Swing

Does having a nice golf swing pay off? One of my best students, Sherry, has a beautiful, smooth, flowing golf swing. When Sherry first started lessons, she was nervous and uptight about playing. As she progressed and became more relaxed, her swing started taking shape and she worked hard on developing the proper form. Even before she learned to play very well, her swing was receiving compliments. In fact over the years I have benefited from her golf swing because many people who have played with her ended up taking lessons from me. So yes, Sherry's golf swing paid off—for me. It has paid off for her as well, because she has developed a very nice golf game.

What is the full swing? The full swing is the entire swing pattern needed to hit the ball. It is the preparation, force, and follow-through in one complete motion.

How do you perform a full swing? This may be the simplest yet most complicated act in any sport. It is so simple that very young kids can pick it up, and it is so difficult that world-class athletes struggle in their attempts to learn.

The swing as you have seen includes many parts, yet all these parts must be blended into the proper sequence. Anything other than this sequence and the golfer needs to compensate at some point.

My advice for any golfer is that when you are playing, just make the golf swing—do not try to practice. You have only your current ability level, and you can't be any better than you are at that time. When you are practicing, practice the parts of the swing.

Why is my practice swing so good? This is a common question. Most people are able to make a full swing that looks almost professional, but put a ball at their feet and they fall apart. When a person makes a practice swing, they follow the proper sequence and actually make a swing. When a ball is present, things change. They naturally hold the club tighter and swing faster. It becomes more of an attempt to hit. The sequence is then interrupted and a variety of things can happen, not a lot of which are good.

For several years I taught the golf swing indoors, which I am convinced is the most effective place to teach and learn. In this facility we used swing analyzers to record data. This data included club speed and tempo. Almost every time we had a student take a swing without a ball, followed immediately by one with a ball, the difference in speed and tempo was about 10 percent. The swing with the ball was always faster.

This makes for a perplexing problem. Beginner and intermediate golfers need to make a practice swing, but if they make a nice swing without a ball, it rarely helps the cause and more often lessens the odds for a good shot. The answer? Don't make a good practice swing. How you accomplish that will be described in the Full Swing Practice section in which we will tie all of this together.

Can you play well without a good full swing? I have seen a lot players who can play reasonably well with poor form. Generally these people are limited in their potential and even in their present ability. Usually they can play a familiar course quite well, but put them on a difficult course and they fall apart. Yes, they can play okay, but I think they are capable of playing much better.

Full Swing Practice

Finally this is a practice in which we will make the golf shot more important than the mechanics. A simple way to do this is to make use of the practice swing. Very rarely can a person make a full practice swing and follow it up with a golf shot in which the swing is as good. The reason, as illustrated above, is that you will swing faster when a ball is present as well as hold the club more tightly. When the swing is faster, you are not in the same position at the same time with the two swings. So the feeling of the practice swing and real swing are different.

The answer to making an effective practice swing is to create one that has the feeling of a good golf swing. In doing so it means that the practice swing probably will not look like a good swing—in fact it may look like a poor swing. The purpose of a practice swing is not to look nice but to remind you how to make the golf swing.

Otherwise you will forget the proper motions and return to what is natural for you.

Drill 14—Push Practice Swing. Line up at least a foot farther away from the ball than normal. Take two practice swings but not full swings. Instead you will substitute the Push Drill for the practice swings. Let these two swings influence your swing enough so that when you approach the ball and make a full swing, the ball will travel to the right. It may draw back slightly, but the most important feature is that it makes you swing inside out.

Drill 15—Short Combination Practice Swing. Line up in the same position as the previous drill, and take two practice swings that are the same length and same direction as the Push Drill. But this time add the hand and arm rotation that we used in the Hook Drill. Do not follow through any farther than the Push Drill. Once you have made the second practice swing, step up and hit the shot. If you make the practice swings the way it is suggested, they should influence your swing enough to use the proper underlying fundamentals without thought.

Practice Routine. Again use three golf balls for this routine. With ball one use the Push Drill with the addition of hand and arm action and actually hit the ball. With ball two step back and make two practice swings using the short combination practice. Once you have completed the practice swing, step up and hit the shot. When hitting the shot you should forget everything. You either have it or you don't, and that should be the way you approach any golf shot. If you have let the practice swings do their job, the feeling should stay with you long enough to execute the shot. With this shot do not try for any specific target. Watch the flight of the ball, however, and judge the distance that it travels in the air. With ball three pick out a target. Step behind the ball and view the target, address the ball, then move back and take two short combination practice swings. Move up to the ball and swing. Ideally it will travel toward the target!

This is a seven-swing practice plan. Five of the swings have a thought with them, the Push Drill and the two practice swings before each full swing. On the full swings you are just making a big relaxed swing and it is hoped that all of your preparation will pay off.

As you travel to the golf course now you have a way to transfer your skill. You obviously can't do the drill on the course, but you certainly can make the practice swings. Many times people practice at the driving range and develop a nice rhythm as they hit ball after ball. When they travel to the golf course, they don't have the luxury of hitting one ball after another and that rhythm is destroyed. This is a method to play on the course exactly the way you practice.

Our practice to this point has been primarily with a No. 7 iron. You should now start using all of your clubs. Make sure to use the drills no matter which club you are using. Try to develop a sense for distance that each club will deliver the ball. Remember, the swing stays the same no matter which club you are using. There are only subtle differences in the stance caused by the length of the club. You will stand either closer to the ball or farther, changing your posture. With the wood clubs you will stand farther from the ball as well as play the ball more toward your left heel.

As you will see in the upcoming chapters there is more to playing the game than just the golf swing. But as we know, there is much satisfaction in striking that great golf shot. Review the previous chapters, become proficient with the drills, and start working toward the golf course.

Drill Checklist

Use the following checklist to rate yourself on your ability to perform the drills. Some drills will be easier for you than others. Just keep in mind that if you want to have a proficient golf swing, you must be able to perform the parts of the swing in order to perform the full swing.

.Drill	Poor	Good	Great
1. Short Swing Drill			
2. Three-Ball Drill			
3. Full Swing Drill			
4. Push Drill			
5. Long Push Drill			
6. Hook Drill			
7. Combination Drill			
8. Takeaway Drill			
9. Backswing Completion Drill			
10. One-Leg Drill			
11. Short Downswing			
12. Short Follow-Through and Return			
13. Full Follow-Through and Return			
14. Push Practice Swing Drill			
15. Short Combination Practice Swing Drill			

Chapter

Putting

The old saying "It's not rocket science" certainly applies to golf. Or does it? Arguably the best short game and putting instructor at one time worked for NASA. The inventor of the Ping putter and founder of Ping Golf Company was an engineer. But in keeping with the purpose of this book I am not going into great detail in describing the putting stroke. The intent is to help you become a good enough putter to allow you to play a comfortable game with the time you have to practice. If you desire to become a very good or great player, you really need to understand the motion and devote a high percentage of your time to practicing this aspect of the game.

This is the part of the game where the playing field is more equal. You may not physically be capable of hitting a 300-yard drive, but you can become consistent with a putter from three feet or adept at rolling the ball from thirty feet close enough to the hole to make your next putt.

I grew up a block from a miniature golf course. The owner was a friend of the family, and even when I was very young, he would pay me to work in the shop in the afternoons. There was rarely any business so I would play, sometimes ten rounds in a day. The different shots, speed of the carpet, and constant practice all helped me develop a solid and imaginative putting stroke.

Not always but more often than not great players are great putters. Recently a television commentator gave an incredible statistic on Tiger Woods. I can't remember the exact number of three-foot putts he had attempted over several years, but it was well over a thousand, and in all of those attempts he had missed only one putt. To me that is more amazing than his phenomenal ball striking. If not the greatest he is one of the great putters of all time.

There are different grips and different strokes, but if you study the great putters, you see more similarities than differences. Also in common is the fact that they have spent a good deal of time working on putting. This is the part of the game that can be practiced away from the golf course, and I would guess that many of our golf professionals have some type of carpet or other means that they can use for practice at home.

The putting stroke differs from the golf swing in that it is a much straighter movement. In other words the head of the putter travels on a straight line away from the target and toward the target after impact. The length of the putt dictates exactly how straight of a line the putter travels.

During the golf swing you need movement from your body to attain power, from your legs to your arms. In the putting stroke we want to be steadier. Force is not the object; accuracy is. You want the face of the putter to point toward the target as long as possible, thus the straight back-and-through movement of the putter face.

To achieve this consistent putter face position, you can do several things mechanically that are different from the golf swing. Again there are variations of the following that you may want to adapt for yourself.

Technique

The Grip. The conventional putting grip is called the *reverse overlap*. Take a normal grip, whether it is baseball, overlap, or interlock. For a right-handed golfer simply place your left index finger on the outside and down the fingers of your right hand. This puts some tension in the left wrist and usually makes the stroke firmer. A wristy or loose motion is a killer in the putting stroke. Often on television they show a close-up of Tiger Woods's putting grip, which is exactly the one I have described. The left hand low, belly putters, claw grip, and long putters are simply attempts to make the stroke quieter.

Without a quiet motion not only is it difficult to be consistent but you could develop the yips. You may have heard this expression at some time. Although it may be funny to watch your opponent suffer with this malady, it certainly is not a fun thing to go through. A yip is almost like an explosion of your muscles just as you are about to make contact with a putt. Usually it results in a short putt and the ball sailing way past the cup.

A friend of mine who passed away a few years ago suffered from the yips. Len was a wonderful ball striker, and when his putting was on, he was as good as anyone. But when it was bad, it was a horrible thing to watch. Len qualified for the U.S. Senior Open one year. He had putted very well in the qualifier and planned to arrive at the Open well in advance of the spectators and big-name tour players.

This would give him time to practice and develop confidence on the greens.

The tournament was held in Des Moines, Iowa, one of the best golf states in the country. Fans love to watch, so when he arrived at the course on early Monday morning, thousands of spectators were already in attendance as well as many of the top senior pros. He was very nervous in the practice round and the yips came back. Later he told me his only chance to make a putt was to close his eyes. This was a terrible way to have to play in a major championship. Although his ball striking was good, it was not enough, and he missed the cut.

The stance. It is probably a good idea to have your feet a little wider than a normal golf stance since you really do not need foot or leg action. I recommend a stance in which your feet, hips, and shoulders are square or parallel to the target line. You may stand erect if you like, but watch most of the good putters and they seem to bend over from the waist, with maybe a slight bend in the knees. Your eyes should be over the target line, not necessarily over the ball.

The stroke. The stroke is a straight back-and-through motion generated by the upper arms and shoulders. Remember, the legs remain steady, your head is still, and your hands are passive. The length of the stroke is dictated by the length of the putt. The backstroke and follow-through should be about the same, with the follow-through maybe slightly longer.

Lining up. A golfer could master a perfect putting stroke, but what good would it do if he or she were lined up in the wrong direction? Yet lining up may be more difficult than a perfect putting stroke. Why should it be so difficult to line up? The reason is the position of your eyes. When you are standing alongside the ball, your eye closest to the target is usually above the other eye. This creates an illusion and makes it difficult to line up square to the target. If would be much easier to stand directly behind the ball as in croquet. That way your eyes would be horizontal to the ground. That is against the rules in golf.

So how do you get around this? Hours of practice from a poor stance will eventually lead to a poor stroke. If you line up to the right, you have to pull the ball, and if you line up to the left, you must push the ball back to the target. Neither way is a very consistent method for the golf course. During practice you could use some tool that has either a line or straight edge. There are many such items on the market, most of which are very good. Unfortunately you are not allowed these conveniences during a round of golf.

You can do what the better players do. They either use the name of the ball or draw a straight line on the ball. When they place the ball down and remove the marker (you are allowed to pick the ball up when you are on the putting green), they line the name or the line toward the target, then line the putter up with the name or line, and finally line themselves up with the putter. It's completely legal under the rules and definitely helpful.

Reading a green. I have mentioned a couple of times that you line up to the target, and for the most part the hole is considered the target. However, on the putting green that is rarely the case. This is simply because greens are not often perfectly flat. Almost always there is some type of hill, undulation, or slant between your ball and the cup. This means that it will curve or break one way or the other. It is up to you to determine how much the ball will curve. This what we call reading a green or guessing which way and how much it will curve.

There are many factors involved in this guess. The slope of the ground is probably the biggest factor, but the texture of the grass, when and how closely the green was mowed, and even the wind all have a big effect. Like I said, it is just a guess, but the more you practice and gain experience, the better guesser you become.

Pre-putt routine. At least as important if not more important than during the golf swing is to develop a pre-putt routine. A routine should be one that you are comfortable with and one that prepares you for the upcoming putt. The following is an example. Start off looking at the putt from behind the ball where your eyes are level. This will give you the best view to read the green. Pick out a spot a foot or so in front of the ball on the target line. Remember, the target line is not necessarily at the hole, depending on the break of the green.

Use the brand name or a line on the ball and set it up pointing at your target. Do all of this from behind the ball where your eyes won't play tricks on you. Move alongside the ball, using the name to help you line up. Make two practice strokes to get the feel for distance, then step to the ball and putt.

Shortly after turning fifty I was playing in a mini tour event for Senior Golfers. It was at Pala Mesa Golf Course in Fallbrook, California. The greens there are very tricky, and I putted well in both rounds of the two-day tournament. I came to the last hole with a two-shot lead and a chance to win my first tournament of any significance. I played it very safe and simply needed to two putt from ten feet for the win. All of a sudden my putter wouldn't move and my hands felt frozen. All sorts of bad thoughts went through my mind. For some reason I had the presence of mind to back off and begin my routine again. Somehow the putt came to rest about a foot and a half from the hole. I was more terrified with that putt, but again, using the routine, I was able to make the putt and won the tournament and a nice check. My putting routine literally saved me from myself.

Putting Practice

There are many different ways to practice putting, and you need to develop a system that fits your personality and time frame. The following are just a few ideas. Regardless of how you practice, make it on a consistent basis. When you go to hit balls on the range, make sure you stop at the putting green.

Drill 1. Practice short putts from about three feet (approximately the length of your putter). Become good at this length, because at most holes you will have this putt. Line the name of the ball up, or use a range ball with stripes or some mechanical method to ensure your stroke goes straight back and straight through.

Drill 2. This drill has been made famous by Phil Mickelson, but I remember using the exercise well before he was born. Put ten balls in a circle around the hole, each ball three feet away, as in the previous drill. See how many out of the ten you can make. If you are consistent in making six of ten, then you are a 60 percent putter from that distance, which is only fair. Make this part of your practice routine and try to get that percentage up.

Drill 3. Move back to thirty feet and hit ten putts, trying to have the ball end up within three feet. If you can do this with a high percentage and are a high percentage putter from three feet, then you have a good chance of shooting decent scores on the golf course.

Practice Routine. After you have done the above three drills, take one ball and pretend you are playing a round of golf. On the first hole try a four-foot putt for par, on the next hole a twenty-foot putt for birdie, and so on. Make it realistic for your ability level. Very good golfers often use these imaginary games. In fact I have won the U.S. Open many times on a practice green.

Home Practice—If you have a smooth area at home, use it to work on your stroke, especially your stance. There are many different types of mats you can buy that actually have a regulation-size cup. Try to practice with some visual aid such as a line or some physical aid. There are many such items on the market.

One of my favorite putting stories happened several years ago at the PGA Tour's Las Vegas Invitational. My student Ed had participated in the event for several years. He was a 21 handicap, but by paying the $3,500 entry fee he was allowed to compete with the 450 amateurs who made up that part of the field.

The format was for three rounds, with the amateurs cut to the low twenty-four at the end of the third round. On the final day each would be paired with the corresponding pro, low pro with low amateur.

Ed was determined to make the cut and employed me as his caddie. We worked hard on his game for several months and it paid off. His ball striking was good for the first three rounds; he putted especially well and he made the cut. I believe he was thirteenth place out of 450 entrants.

On the final round we were paired with Mark McCumber. Mark was a fine striker of the ball and he hit the ball extremely well on that particular day, but he could not make a putt to save his life. Ed on the other hand was nervous from the crowds and television coverage, and he was awful at hitting the ball. But Ed could putt, and he did a great job making several midrange putts.

He came to the last hole, where the second shot was a very difficult one over water. The green was surrounded by spectators, so Ed was understandably nervous. Somehow he managed to get the ball on the green, although it was about fifty feet from the hole. His putt was going straight downhill toward the same water he had just cleared. I was afraid that if he putted the ball a little too hard, it would roll into the lake.

Nothing prepared me for what he did. He knocked the ball directly into the cup for a birdie. The crowd went wild. Mark McCumber had a funny look on his face. And Ed will have a memory to cherish the rest of his life.

Chapter

8

Short Game

The syllabus for my class at Cal State–Fullerton said that on a particular day we would work on the short game. Most members of the class were disappointed when we did not actually go on the golf course and play a short game of golf.

What is the short game? This is the scoring part of the game. It is a variety of shots hit with less than a full swing and with the intention of getting the ball close to or in the hole. This is usually the area of the game that determines whether a golfer is what we call a good player or not. Good players inevitably have good short games. A golfer can make up for many mistakes through their short game play.

What constitutes the short game? There are many shots, but for our purposes in this book we will focus on wedge play and chip shots.

How much should a person practice the short game? Because short shots constitute a high percentage of the shots a golfer plays on the golf course, their practice should be in proportion. Rarely do I see it happen, with the exception of the better players. You can have a good or even a great score with bad shots and a good short game. But it is most difficult to have even a good score with great shots and a poor short game.

Is it difficult to develop a short game? It is not easy because there are thousands of situations such as different lengths, different conditions, and different lies. It takes many practice hours. However, you can normally find a place to practice for free. Most golf courses have a putting green and usually some type of short game area.

Is technique important? Technique certainly makes it easier to be consistent and its importance should not be diminished, but it is probably not as important as in the full swing.

Chip Shots

When you are on the green, you putt the ball with a putter. You don't have to use this club, but it is the one best suited for the shot. When you are just off the green and the grass is cut short and smooth, a putter would probably be a great choice. In fact there are occasions when a putter would be an efficient club to use from many yards off the green.

But what do you do when you are very close to the green yet the grass between your ball and the green is long, fluffy, or uneven? Then it becomes difficult to judge how hard to hit the ball. Will the grass slow it up or not? In this circumstance we will term the shot that we use a *chip shot*. The club you use is up to you. I would suggest that you begin with a No. 7 iron. You may choose another club to use for this shot; that is certainly up to you.

Like a putting stroke. The technique for a chip shot is the same as a putting stroke. Many players use the putting grip as well. The major difference in this shot is that the club is usually longer than a putter and you must stand slightly farther from the ball. A rule of thumb may be that you have the ball travel about one-fourth of the distance in the air and roll the remaining three fourths. That will change with the slope of the green but can be used as a guideline. Make this a stroke and allow the loft of the club to get the ball airborne don't try to help or lift the ball up. It isn't necessary and will destroy the shot.

Chip Shot Practice

Drill 1. On the driving range simply practice the technique of the chip shot. Don't worry about a target as much as how far the ball goes in the air with a certain length backstroke.

Drill 2. At a practice green take eleven golf balls. Chip each one toward the same hole from the same location. Take away the closest five balls and the five farthest from the hole. The last ball left will give you an indication of how good you are with the chip shot.

Drill 3. At a practice green take a ball, the club you chip with, and a putter. Lay the ball close to the green, select a hole, and chip the ball toward the target. Putt the ball from the position that it comes to rest. Your goal is to get the ball "up and in" with no more than two shots. Repeat this from different parts of the green and to different holes.

Routine. Make at least one of the above drills part of your regular practice routine.

Wedge Play

Many golf professionals carry at least three and sometimes four different wedges in their golf bags. Because the rules allow only fourteen clubs in the bag, this is a high percentage for any type of club, which shows you the value that they place on wedge play.

Why are the wedges so important? Wedges are important for a variety of reasons. First the wedge is a club that is critical to playing the game well for scoring purposes. Not only can you take advantage of opportunities to score, but good wedge play will allow you to make up for poor shots. Many rounds have been saved via good wedge play.

Second, a wedge is a relatively easy club to hit with, so you should be able to gain confidence in your ball striking. Distance is not an issue, so it allows you to swing more easily and develop rhythm. It is a great club to use to warm up and to help you relax if you are having trouble with your ball striking. Therefore it is a good club to use for practice.

What types of wedges are available? There are many different types with a variety of lofts. The standard pitching wedge usually has around 47 degrees of loft, and wedges go all the way up to and sometimes even exceed 60 degrees. As you progress in the game, experiment and find out which wedges fit best.

Although there are many different types of pitch shots, we are going to focus on just three: the pitch and run, the cut shot, and the knockdown. Each has a purpose, and you need to know how and when to use the proper one.

Pitch and Run. Of all the shots that you could practice, this is probably the most important for a couple of reasons. Number one is the fact that there often is the opportunity to use this shot on the golf course during a round of golf. Number two, the mechanics of the pitch and run are similar to the golf swing. So you are killing two birds with one stone. You are practicing something you need on the golf course and your golf swing at the same time.

Because distance is not required, the swing is a little more relaxed. With the loft of the golf club and shorter shaft it is relatively easy to hit, so you can develop confidence and rhythm. In fact if you attend a professional tournament and go to the driving range, you will see the pros warm up with the wedge first to develop a rhythm. Oftentimes after the round the same players will be back on the range using the wedge to get their rhythm back.

The mechanics of the pitch and run are very similar to the regular golf swing. The golfer takes the same stance. The length of the backswing is dictated by the length of the golf shot. The longer the distance the ball needs to travel, the longer the swing. The weight shifts on the downswing and the follow-through are slightly longer than the backswing. The right arm crosses over the left arm in the same manner as a normal full golf swing.

The ball flight is not very high. One mistake that beginner and intermediate golfers make is that they try to make the ball land and stop close to the target. This is very difficult in a short shot. The pitch and run means the ball will travel in the air, but then when it hits the ground, it will roll. This is a much more relaxed way to play a short shot than trying to make the ball stick.

Several factors control the height of the shot. The length of the swing is the biggest contributor. The longer the swing, the more distance the ball travels in the air, the more backspin imparted on the ball, and the less roll. The shorter the swing, the lower the ball trajectory and the more roll. It is up to you to practice different-length shots and develop the proper swing for the distance required.

Another factor is the club that is used. The pitching wedge, gap wedge, sand wedge, and lob wedge will all give different heights to the shot with the same swing.

The position that you play the ball in your stance will change the trajectory somewhat. In the center of the stance like a regular shot will give normal height, farther forward will give more height, and farther back will create a lower shot. Just remember, until you make a full swing, this shot has only a minimum amount of backspin and the ball will roll or run regardless of the club.

Cut Shot. The cut shot is actually making use of a poor golf swing. It is a swing in which the club travels outside in, and there is restricted hand action. Often in lessons I teach students this shot, then videotape their attempt as well as a regular golf swing with a longer club. It is not unusual to have the two swings look very similar. This is not a good thing, because a powerful and effective swing would look very different from the cut shot. But it does prove a point: that a natural, easy swing to make is the cut shot. It is one that doesn't take much time to learn and will surface in a full golf swing if you don't make the effort to avoid it.

What is the purpose of the cut shot? Cutting across the ball deliberately allows the golfer to hit the ball hard and not have it travel very far. It is a shot that is needed in certain situations and is also the mechanics of the sand shot. Please read that first statement again, because if you are lacking distance in your full swings, more than likely you are cutting across the ball.

The pitch and run shot is well and good for most situations. As I mentioned, it is great practice. But what happens when you are close to the target and need to make the ball travel higher and land more softly? An example would be to land the ball just over a sand trap when the pin is on that side of the green.

The premise of this book has been to effectively learn the golf swing you need to swing on an inside-out pattern. Now we are going to hit a shot in which we need to change our view. To make the ball have height and little distance you need to swing outside-in.

This is accomplished by opening the stance. In other words instead of standing with the feet, hips, and shoulders parallel to the target line, the right-handed golfer aligns to the left. The body is almost facing the target. The face of the club is one we call open to the stance, but it is actually square to the target line. The path of the club head follows the stance, in other words outside in or cutting across the ball. This puts a sidespin on the ball that gives it height but not distance.

To keep the ball going to the left of the target or the direction of the club path, this is a swing in which we block our hand action. In other words it is not only permissible to use the chicken wing follow-through, but almost a requirement. This takes the distance off the shot and starts the ball toward the target even though you are lined up pointing and swinging to the left.

For anyone other than an expert player the cut shot is one in which the ball needs to be sitting up on the ground in a good lie. That means there needs to be a little cushion under the ball. Even with a good lie it is a risky shot, but during a round of golf sometimes it is the only choice you have.

Is the cut shot used in the sand? Watch the golfers on television and you will see that they stand open and use the cut shot. There are a few differences in playing out of the sand. First the golfer doesn't make contact with the golf ball. The golf club hits the sand behind the ball and the explosion of the sand throws the ball out of the trap. This is actually a fairly easy shot in the fact that there is a margin of error. In other words you don't have to hit the sand in a precise spot.

Contact with the sand a little more behind the ball makes it roll more; contact a little closer to the ball makes it stop faster.

Second, it is almost always a full swing. Distance control comes from how open the stance is. The more open it is, the shorter distance the ball will travel; the more square, the farther the ball will travel.

The key to sand play is confidence. The very first golf lesson I gave was at Ridge Country Club in Chicago. Mr. B. was a wonderful old gentleman who was terrified of the sand, and thus he had no confidence. We worked for a long time, his mechanics were not bad, and finally he was able to at least extract the ball from the bunker.

The next weekend there was a fun tournament at the club. It had special rules, one of which was that at some point in the round the competitors were allowed to throw the ball. On the fourteenth hole Mr. B. hit the ball into the sand trap. He had not used his throwing option yet, so it was a perfect time. He picked the ball up and threw it as hard as he could. However, the ball slipped out of his hand and lodged under the lip of the bunker and into an impossible position. I decided then that Mr. B. was the worst sand player of all time. He couldn't even throw the ball out of the trap. Confidence is the key to sand play. Develop the cut shot on the grass, then use it in the sand.

The Knockdown. Many times television announcers say a player is going to "knock down the shot." What they are saying is that the golfer is going to arrest his follow-through and make the ball travel lower. It is a great shot for wind and certain other situations such as underneath a tree. I am convinced that the best way to learn this shot is with the wedges.

The knockdown is a shot that can be very accurate. It is also a shot that can be used when the ball is sitting in a bad lie. The mechanics of the shot are to play the ball back in the stance. Move the hands forward, thus reducing the loft off the golf club. The stroke is to take the club straight back and straight through. This motion limits the length of the backswing. The backswing is then shorter than normal, but the follow-through is even shorter than the backswing. The face of the club has pointed toward the target throughout the stroke, making this a very accurate shot. Since there is no hand action with this shot, distance is limited.

Wedge Practice

There are so many different short game situations, a golfer could practice countless hours and never have the same shot. You can have good lies, bad lies, short grass, long grass, uphill, or downhill. The list goes on and on. So how do you practice all the different shots? The truth is you don't. You learn and practice the basic shots. Do the best you can with what you have. The more experience, the better you will become at deciding which shot to play in different situations.

Over the years in teaching short game to classes I have learned a few things to do and not to do. If you are working in a practice area where there is little room, make sure of the safety of those around you. I have had a student hit a line drive into a restroom and a pitch shot that went over the roof of the clubhouse. I have seen a full swing on a ten-foot shot and a ball bounce off a wall and hit a police car. Fortunately the ball bounced from a different direction than from our class and the policeman didn't even look our way. Just be careful!

Pitch and Run. This practice can actually take the place of the nine-ball drill. In fact this is great practice; as I mentioned earlier, you will be killing several birds with one stone. When you become proficient with the wedge, you will develop confidence and thus relaxation. It is a great way to warm up and develop rhythm for the day, whether you are practicing or playing. It is something you need on the golf course.

Drill 1. Stretch and take a few full swings without a ball. Then place three balls on the ground or mat. With the first ball take one-third of a swing or about knee high; ball two take two-thirds of a swing, club shaft pointing at the sky; and with ball three take a full swing. With this drill there is no precise target. You simply are trying to make solid contact with the ball. Use different wedges and become accustomed to the loft and distance that each will produce.

Drill 2. Use the same sequence as the first drill, but this time, pick out targets. Try to judge the exact distance so that you can develop a feel for the length of the swing you need. Again use the different wedges.

Drill 3. You need to move to a practice green for this exercise. Take eleven golf balls and hit all from the same location, trying for the same target. After you have hit all eleven, pick up the five closest to the hole and the five farthest from the target. The ball that is left is a good indication of your ability.

Drill 4—Cut Shot Practice. You need some room for this shot. It is wise not to practice this in a small area; the driving range would probably work best. Because you are practicing a bad swing, make this just a small portion of the practice. Use either a sand wedge or lob wedge for this shot.

Drill 5—Sand Shots. You need to find a practice sand trap. Not every golf course has one available for the public, but many do. Once you are proficient at getting the ball out of the bunker—and it simply takes a little practice to get the knack—try the eleven-ball exercise outlined in Drill 3.

Drill 6—Knockdown Practice. Try this shot with varying lengths. Start with a five-yard sho,t then ten, fifteen, and so on. You can do this practice on the driving range or on a practice green.

Practice Routine. Begin with pitch and run shots, one short, one medium, and one three-quarters. During this time try to establish how far the ball goes in the air with each swing. Vary golf clubs and observe how the loft affects the distance. Repeat this sequence until you think you are developing a feel for the distance. Do the same thing with the cut shot and the knockdown shot.

Home Practice. This is difficult unless you have an area in which you can hit shots—maybe a nearby park or your backyard. Watch out for neighbors. They get grouchy when a titleist ends up in their living room via a window. That advice comes from personal experience.

Chapter

9

⭐ ETIQUETTE

Playing an enjoyable round of golf with others who are courteous and have an appreciation for the game makes for a very fun day. Playing the game with someone who is not courteous can be a miserable experience. It detracts from your game as well as the spirit of the great game of golf. Make sure you are not that person!

I don't know how many private lessons I have given over the past thirty-five years, but it has been a considerable number. In all that time I have had many requests for lessons on different aspects of the game but never one for etiquette. Almost always the request is for something to do with ball striking. Understandably everyone wants to improve the way they hit the ball. Yet more than likely golfers will be judged by the way they conduct themselves on the course almost as much as by their ability to hit the ball.

What is etiquette? It is your observance of the code for correct behavior in respect to the other players, and to the course itself. The purpose is to reduce the probability of injury, to speed up play, and to enjoy the game.

How difficult is it to learn the etiquette or manners that a golfer needs to play the game? It is not that difficult if the golfer is willing to take a small amount of time to practice these important rules of conduct. These are not rules of the game; there is no penalty for violation of etiquette. But more than likely as you play you will be judged by your golf etiquette.

How important is it to learn golf etiquette? At Cal State–Fullerton we put a significant amount of importance on etiquette. We practice the etiquette that is required and students are given an etiquette test at the end of the semester. With many business majors in the classes it is easy to point out that if you are playing with your boss or a client, you do not want to offend that person. This could happen quite easily without knowing the rules of etiquette.

It is very difficult if a golfer has not been on the golf course to understand certain mechanics of etiquette no matter how well they are explained. However, if that golfer can be made aware intellectually, then when they go out to play for the first time they will have a leg up on the proper courtesies of the game. Ideally that first time will be with friends or family members who have played and are versed in the essential etiquette of the game.

Is etiquette an essential element? In my opinion it is as important as the golf swing. Please don't discount this critical part of the game. I have noticed over the past few years that etiquette on the golf course, much the same as in society, has slipped a notch. It is important to do your part to keep this sport one that is played by ladies and gentlemen.

Basic Rules of Etiquette

Fore! When this old word of the game is yelled, it doesn't mean hello. There is an errant golf ball and it's on the way, so duck. Even though it can be very embarrassing to hit a poor golf shot on the golf course, *fore* should be yelled as loudly as possible. Many court cases have been won by golfers who were struck by a golf ball and had not been given fair warning.

Be ready to play. Arrive at the golf course early. If you have a 10A.M. time, that doesn't mean be at the pro shop at 10. It means you should be warmed up and ready to hit the ball at your appointed time. Give yourself time and it will be easier to relax. Hit some practice balls and a few putts. It is difficult to relax if you are rushed.

Slow play. This is a detriment to the game. You should be ready when it is your turn to play. You can decide which club to use as you approach the ball. Even when riding in a cart, begin calculating your distance before you arrive at the ball. When on the fairway the clubs should be kept close at hand. On the putting green clubs should be placed in an area between the hole and the next tee. Don't leave individual clubs spread around the green. Pro shops are full of lost clubs that players forgot and left behind.

We certainly want to emulate golf professionals in the way they swing and strike the ball. Often these players are very slow and deliberate when they hit the golf ball, but they are almost always ready to play when it is their turn, and they do the proper things to speed up play.

Taking care of the course. All golfers are responsible for helping to maintain the golf course. Repairing divots on the fairway, fixing ball marks on the green, and raking footprints out of traps are not only considerate things to do but common sense. It is very discouraging to hit the ball into the middle of the fairway and find it lying in a divot that wasn't repaired. If you make a divot, which is simply the turf displaced by your golf club, then put it back in that area of the torn-up ground. Many golf courses provide a sand and grass seed mixture for that purpose. It may be in a bottle lying in the fairway or attached to a golf cart.

For the average golfer sand shots can be a struggle, but when the ball is lying in an unraked footprint, it is a disaster. Use a rake that is provided and is usually lying next to the trap. When you enter the sand trap, enter from the lowest point and rake the sand in that direction. This polite action takes only a few seconds.

When a ball lands on the green, it generally makes a dent called a *ball mark*. If this is not fixed, it more than likely will turn brown and take a few weeks to heal. There is also a chance that a golfer playing in a group behind you may not see the mark as he or she putts, and this will make the ball veer off line if it rolls over the mark. Use a tee or an actual ball mark tool to lift up the edges of the mark. Then take your putter and smooth the repaired area until it is flat.

Avoid the putting line. Probably there is no more flagrant violation of etiquette than this one. This will get a fellow golfer's dander up faster than anything. On the putting green there is an intended line extending from the golf ball to the cup. This line is sacred, and if someone inadvertently steps on it, often they leave a footprint. Even if there is no footprint, it is very distracting to the golfer who needs to putt. Always be aware of the position of your playing companion's golf ball. Walk around their line of putt to putt or mark your ball. This takes awareness on your part, but I can't emphasize it enough!

I have played with many people who have walked across either my line or a playing companion's line. The inclination is to think that the person is either rude or worse. In other words, not being aware of this rule of etiquette is not a penalty in strokes but could have different, more severe consequences.

Marking the ball. The rules of golf allow the golfer to pick up the ball when it is on the putting green. To do this you must first put down behind the ball a small flat object such as a coin to mark the position. We talked in an earlier chapter about lining the ball up for the putting stroke, but just as important a reason would be to move the ball out of another golfer's way. If, when putting, the putter's ball strikes another ball, it is a two-stroke penalty. Even if it is not in the direct path, it may be distracting. You should be in the habit of always marking the ball. Not only is it proper etiquette, but you can clean the ball off as well as line up the name toward the target.

Patti had never been on a course until our class went out one evening. On the first hole I told her to mark her ball, which she didn't know how to do. So I took a quarter and laid it behind the ball and handed the ball to her. When it was her turn, I told her to go ahead and putt. She did—she putted the quarter! The class and I were speechless for a long time.

Standing position. It can be very distracting to see another golfer out of the corner of the eye. Even a shadow can throw someone off. You should be very aware of where you are standing so as not to be distracting or in danger of being hit by a club or ball.

When I attended Western Illinois University, I would beg rides to and from a nearby golf course. An elderly couple who played nearly every afternoon would often give me a ride home. On one occasion I was going to play nine holes with them. On the first hole the lady took a practice swing and hit her husband in the head. This was well over thirty years ago, and I can still remember the sound of her driver making contact with his head. In those days woods were made out of real wood instead of metal, and it was as if she had hit a coconut. Fortunately he was was okay, but it ruined their day.

Order of play. Once all members of the group have teed off, the person to play next is the one farthest from the hole. There are occasional exceptions to this rule, but for the most part for safety and speed of play, golfers should follow this pattern. When you have a very short putt and will not stand in the line of another player, it is permissible to play out of turn. After the first hole whoever had the lowest score on the previous hole has the "honor." So if you had the lowest score on the first hole, you would go first on the second hole.

I have had the opportunity to play with many great players. With only a few exceptions has their etiquette not been exceptional. I can say without a doubt that a good golfer would rather play with a poor player who knows etiquette than with a good player who does not have good etiquette.

Chapter

10

RULES

Play starts from a designated area called the *tee*. You, the golfer, hit the ball with a club until it ends up in a designated hole in the ground called the *cup*. Play ends when eighteen holes have been completed. In the true sense of the game you hit the ball, find it, and then hit it again. But what happens when you lose the ball or find it lodged against a tree or sitting on a sprinkler head? Like every other game there needs to be rules to guide the player through the experience. However, unlike most games golf is self-governing. In other words, if you deserve a penalty, more than likely you have to declare it upon yourself. If you do something wrong, you might be the only one to know it, and it is your obligation to report the infraction.

In the second round of the PGA Tour 2007 Honda Classic a unique event took place. A young tour professional named Mark Wilson called a two-stroke penalty on himself. It was actually a gray area of the rules in which his caddie gave advice to another player. It was unnoticed by almost everyone except Mark. He felt like it was enough of an infraction that it was worthy of the penalty. Although he needed the money, the rules of the game outweighed any greed that he might have felt. He shot a decent score that day and made the cut, but his major accomplishment was in consoling his caddie, who took his mistake quite hard.

Calling a penalty on himself was very noble, and most people don't have the opportunity to rule against themselves when the stakes are that high. But there are many, many people who do the same thing in the game every day. How many people in other sports call fouls on themselves, declare their ball of bounds, or anything else that would cause punishment? I can't think of many. By the way, in a very fitting script Mark played fantastic over the weekend, was able to tie for first place, then won in a playoff with three other competitors.

All sports and games have rules. Golf is unique in that it is a self-governing game. You rule yourself. There are no umpires or referees. In tournament play there are rules officials who roam the golf course to help golfers make decisions about rules, but they are not there to decide plays as in baseball, football, or basketball.

For the most part the golfer must decide the correct course of action. An example was when I was a rules official at a college event. A player in one group had hit the ball in the deep rough. It appeared that he was trying to play out when he made a huge swing but did not hit the ball. He declared to the other players in the group that he was not swinging at the ball, just making a practice stroke. Whether he was or not, only he knew. Even though it upset the other players, I had to rule in his favor, because the rule goes to the intent of hitting the shot, and he said he was not trying to hit the ball.

There are only a few basic rules, but there are thousands of situations where they have been interpreted. I am going to cover the rules you are most likely to encounter during a round of golf. If nothing else at least buy the small USGA rules book and put it in your golf bag.

Common Rules

Out of bounds or lost ball. Most golf courses are clearly marked in terms of what is in bounds and what is out of bounds. It could be anything from white stakes to brick walls. It usually is off the property of the golf course. Sometimes the back of the scorecard lists holes where out-of-bounds occurs. The rule is quite simple. If a ball is out of bounds or lost, you must play another shot from the spot where you just hit the ball. It results in a one-stroke penalty and the loss of distance.

This rule brings in etiquette. If you think the ball may be out of bounds but are not quite sure, it is in everyone's best interest to hit a provisional ball. Once that ball has been played, everyone in the group should help look for the first ball. That saves a trip back to the original spot if the ball is in fact out of bounds or lost. If it is playable, then the provisional ball is picked up as if it were never hit.

It is important to identify your golf ball. Each ball has a number on it for the purpose of identifying your ball in the event there is another ball in the vicinity or you have to look for it. You should go a step further and put a personalized mark of some type on the ball. That way no one can dispute whether it was your ball or not. I put my daughter's initials on my golf balls. I would hesitate to put your real name or phone number just in case they end up in embarrassing places such as a friend's swimming pool or worse.

Hazards. There are water hazards and lateral water hazards. Each one has its own form of penalty and procedure. A water hazard is some form of water usually between you and the hole. A lateral hazard is some form of water generally lying parallel or lateral to the hole. A water hazard is defined by yellow stakes or line, and a lateral hazard is defined by red stakes or lines.

The penalty if you are not able to play the ball out of the hazard is one stroke. The options of play are different. If you lose your ball in a water hazard, you need to determine where the ball entered or crossed the margin of the hazard. Then you must keep that point between yourself and the hole. You can go back as far as you want on a straight line. This is often advantageous when the ground slopes or there is rough that you want to avoid. An example is the twelfth hole at Augusta National where the Masters Golf Tournament is played. When a player hits the ball in the water, he will establish the point of entry and retreat far up the hill trying to find a level lie, a position that allows spin on the ball versus staying closer to the green but having to hit the ball from a down slope.

When your ball finds a lateral water hazard, you are afforded more options. Again you need to find the point of entry. Once you have done so, you may take a drop two club lengths and no closer to the hole from that spot. You also may use the same option as a water hazard. A rarely used choice is to go the other side of the hazard and take two club lengths' relief. Another option available with both is to return to the original position and replay the shot.

The proper way to drop the ball is very important. You must stand with your arm extended and drop the ball from shoulder height. You never drop the ball closer to the hole. If the dropped ball ends up closer to the hole or more than two club lengths from the point that it touched the ground, you must redrop it. If it happens again, you are allowed to replace the ball in the exact spot that it first touched the ground.

Another hazard is a sand trap. This hazard is one in which you have a chance to play the ball out. An important rule in sand play is that you are not allowed to touch the surface with your club before you swing. Doing so is called *testing the surface*, and it incurs a two-stroke penalty. This same rule applies to a water hazard and a lateral hazard if you are lucky enough to have the ball in a position to actually make a swing.

Putting green. There are several rules that govern the putting green. First when your ball rests on the green and you play a stroke, your ball cannot contact the flagstick. If that happens, it is a two-stroke penalty. So make sure the flagstick is taken out of the hole and placed in a position where even an errant putt will not strike it. If you are at a distance where you cannot see the hole, then have someone tend the flag for you and pull it out of the hole when you strike the putt.

You can also get a two-stroke penalty if you are on the putting surface and your ball strikes a playing companion's golf ball. That is why it is important to have a golf ball marked when on the green. Even though it may not appear to be in the way, you should still mark your ball.

It is permissible to fix ball marks on the green. In fact make sure you fix your own. It is not permissible to fix spike marks. Loose impediments such as leaves or sand from a bunker may be removed.

Teeing ground. The entire area is called the *teeing ground*. The place where you begin is often called the *tee box*. Usually defined by markers this area has specific rules. You are allowed to use a tee or peg for the first shot of each hole. You must place the ball between the markers, not in front. You can move the ball up to two club lengths behind the markers. Last, only the ball has to be in this rectangle formed by the markers and two club lengths; you are allowed to stand outside this area.

Obstructions. Golf courses have many situations where man-made objects may interfere with play. Cart paths, sprinkler heads, and protective fences are just three examples of what we term *immovable obstructions*. Whenever you are faced with this situation, the rule that is followed is to move the ball to the nearest point of relief from the obstruction. *Relief* in this case means the nearest point where the object will not interfere with your swing or your stance. You then receive one more additional club length, no closer to the hole. You drop the ball and no penalty is involved.

A common misinterpretation of this rule is that golfers often think they have the right to a better shot. This is not true. The rule allows you relief from swinging at, hitting, or standing on the obstruction. An example would be a cart path. If your ball is on the path but nearer to the rough than the fairway, you must drop the ball in the rough or play it off the cart path. The free drop may not give you the most clear or best chance to advance the ball, but the rule is the rule.

An example was during a playoff for the 2007 Nissan Open at Riviera CC in Los Angeles. Charles Howell hit his tee shot on the tenth hole to the left of the fairway and his ball came to rest on the cart path. According to the rule he was allowed a free drop. However, this drop would have put him under a tree and totally blocked his next shot. He chose to hit the ball off the cart path, which he did without incident, making par and continuing the playoff.

Ground under repair and casual water. In both of these cases you are allowed a free drop. Ground under repair is generally marked by the golf course with lines or ropes and signs. Casual water is any water that is visible either before or after you take a stance. The procedure of play is the same as for an obstruction: nearest point of relief plus one additional club length.

The rules of golf booklet. The United States Golf Association governs all rules in the United States. They have published a small pocket-sized book that every golfer should obtain. This book goes into much more detail than I have done in this chapter. There are literally thousands of situations, and if a golfer cannot find the correct solution in the pocket-size rule book, there are more books called the "Decisions" that go into more intricate detail.

Chapter

GLOSSARY

Countless words, terms, and phrases have been used to describe the game and its many aspects. Some of these are unprintable, and for those you are on your own. The following list comprises some of the common words or phrases that you may need to use as you begin or continue to play.

Ace. A hole in one.

Addressing the ball. Taking a stance and grounding the club.

Apron. The area surrounding the putting green, also called the *fringe*. It is usually mowed closer than the fairway but higher than the green.

Away. The ball lying farthest from the hole. Generally if you are "away," it is your turn to play the shot. There are occasions when this is waived.

Back nine. The last nine holes of an eighteen-hole golf course. On the scorecard often it is labeled as "in."

Best ball. A partner format in which the best score on a hole between the partners is the one recorded on the scorecard.

Birdie. A score of one under par for a hole.

Bogey. A score of one over par for a hole.

Break of a green. The slant or slope of the putting green.

Bunker. Normally a sand trap, which is also considered a hazard; could also be a grass depression, in which case it is probably not considered a hazard.

Casual water. A temporary accumulation of water, except in a water hazard.

Chip shot. A short, low trajectory shot played to the putting green.

Cup. This is a term commonly used for the hole on the putting green. Most of the time a plastic liner is used, which is probably where the word *cup* originated.

Divot. A piece of turf displaced in making a stroke.

Dogleg. A hole in which the fairway curves to the right or left.

Double bogey. A score of two over par for a hole.

Double eagle. A score of three under par for a hole. It is also called an albatross and is a very rare occurrence.

Draw. A ball that curves slightly in flight from right to left for a right-handed golfer.

Driver. The No. 1 wood and other than a putter the golf club with the least amount of loft.

Eagle. A score of two under par for a hole.

Fade. A ball that curves slightly in flight from left to right for a right-handed golfer.

Fairway. The closely mowed route of play between the teeing area and the putting green.

Flagstick. The marker that indicates the location of the hole. Often there are different colors on different greens that show the hole's depth on each green, which helps you determine yardage.

Fore. A warning cry to anyone who might be in the way of a golf shot.

Front nine. The first nine holes of an eighteen-hole course.

Gross score. The actual total score for a round adding up the score from every hole.

Ground under repair. Staked or lined area on which work is being done. A ball coming to rest in such an area may be lifted and dropped in accordance with the rules.

Grounding the club. Placing the sole of the club on the ground in preparation for making the stroke.

Handicap. A method to equalize players of different abilities.

Hazards. Any bunker (sand) or water hazard.

Hole. Two definitions. One is the actual hole cut into the putting green that is the ultimate goal with the ball. The other is the entire area from teeing ground to putting green such as the first hole, the second hole, and so on.

Hole out. To complete the play of a hole by having the ball end up in the bottom of the cup.

Hook. A ball that curves from right to left for a right-hander. It has counterclockwise spin.

Lateral water hazard. A water hazard running parallel to the line of play.

Lie. This word has two meanings. One is the position of the ball on the ground. In a golf club it is the angle of the shaft in relation to the club head.

Line of putt. The line you desire your ball to take after a stroke on the putting green.

Loft of club. The angle of pitch of the club face.

Loose impediments. A natural object, not stationary, growing, or adhering to the ball, such as a leaf, twig, branch, or the like.

Match play. Competition based on scores for each hole rather than total score.

Medal play. Competition by total score, also called stroke play.

Mulligan. Taking a second shot without penalty if the first shot is a poor one. Against the rules and poor etiquette.

Net score. A score resulting from subtraction of the handicap from the gross score.

Obstruction. A man-made or artificial object on the course that may be movable or fixed.

Out of bounds. Ground on which play is prohibited. Generally off the golf course property but not always. Usually marked by out-of-bounds stakes or fences.

Outside agency. Any agency that is not part of the game. This could be anything from a tee marker to a dog that picks up a ball and runs away.

Par. An arbitrary standard of scoring excellence based on the length of a hole, allowing two putts on the putting green.

Penalty stroke. A stroke added to your score under certain rules.

PGA. Professional Golfers' Association of America.

Provisional ball. A second ball played in case the first ball is potentially out of bounds or lost outside a water hazard.

Pull. A shot that travels straight but to the left of the target line (right-hander).

Push. A shot that travels straight but to the right of the target line (right-hander).

Putting green. All the ground of the hole you are playing that is specially prepared for putting.

Rough. The areas bordering the fairway in which the grass, weeds, and so on are allowed to grow higher than the fairway, sometimes substantially.

Royal and Ancient Golf Club of St. Andrews, Scotland (The R and A). The governing body of golf in Great Britain and most of the world.

Rub of the green. When a ball is in motion and is accidentally deflected or stopped by an outside agency. It could be either good luck or bad luck.

Sand trap. A bunker filled with sand.

Scramble. A format of play in which all members of the group are a team. Each member tees off, then the player whose ball is in the best position is selected. All players then play the second shot from that position. This continues for every shot until the ball is in the hole. Very popular format for charity events.

Slice. A shot that curves to the right for a right-handed player. The ball has clockwise spin for a right-handed player.

Tee. The starting place for a hole. The teeing ground. Also the peg on which you are allowed to place the ball for the first shot on each hole.

Tee markers. The markers placed on the tee to indicate where play is to begin on each hole.

United States Golf Association (USGA). Governing body of golf in the United States.

Winter rules. Special local rules that permit the ball to be moved to a better lie on the fairway.

Concluding Thoughts

"To exalt the humble and to humble the exalted." I have always thought that this Bible verse is a great description of the game of golf. How many times do we think that we've "got it" only to have the next shot blow up in our face?

This has happened to me countless times. One that sticks out the most in my mind was on a trip to Scotland. My favorite course in the world is the Old Course at St. Andrews. One of my goals has always been to shoot a very good score on that sacred golf course. I have studied the course and played it several times.

Finally I had the opportunity to play the course during a period when I was playing extremely well. The day of the round I got up early and walked a mile to a field to warm up; there were no driving ranges available in those days. I was as ready for that round as any in my life. My tee shot from the first hole almost made the Swilcan Burn in front of the green. If you have ever been to St. Andrews, you know this was a good start. All day long I hit the ball the way I intended, and any bad shots were only marginally bad. Walking up the eighteenth hole, which is a thrill in itself, I had mixed feelings. My old Scottish caddie put it best: "Laddie I love the way you strike the ball, but your putting makes me sick to me stomach." In working so hard on one part of the game I had totally neglected another, and I paid for it that day.

Does it ever all come together? Sometimes, but even if it doesn't, much of the fun is in trying. The golf swing and the entire game is a never-ending search. No matter who you are or how good you become, there is always room for improvement. I have never met the golfer who is satisfied with his or her game for any length of time.

That is the wonderment behind playing and certainly the fascination behind teaching this great game.

About the Author

Jim Howe began playing golf in 1961. Since then, the thousands of rounds, hundreds of tournaments, countless hours of practice, and just passion for the game have all given him a great background for teaching the game. He has continued tournament play throughout his career, winning more than thirty mini tour events after the age of fifty.

As important as playing has been for the past thirty-five years, teaching has been more of his primary focus, starting at Ridge Country Club in Chicago, then moving west to California in the late '70s. It was at his first California stop, Newport Beach G.C., where he began using video during lessons. Around the same time he began teaching large classes at a local community college. The feedback from watching the video and from student comments, particularly the large groups, began shaping him into a teacher, not just someone who knew the golf swing.

In 1980 he took the position as golf coach at Cal State University–Fullerton, which also gave him the opportunity to teach classes as a member the physical education staff. This staff position is one that he still holds today, although it is now called the kinesiology department. The experience of coaching Division One players and teaching college classes as well as returning to school to further his education helped him continue to develop his method, style, and format.

Attempting to follow the footsteps of the famous teachers Earnest Jones and Percy Boomer he taught indoors for several years. It was during this time that he developed a methodology that used a comparative analysis. This has become a very popular format in modern instruction.

At the present he can be found teaching classes at Cal State University–Fullerton. He also teaches private and group lessons at a public golf course in Brea, California.

Jim can be reached by e-mail at jhowe2@aol.com.

CPSIA information can be obtained at www.ICGtesting.com
Printed in the USA
BVOW010030041212

307147BV00003B/264/A